OURSELVES ALONE

OURSELVES ALONE

Women's Emigration
from Ireland
1885-1920

JANET A. NOLAN

THE UNIVERSITY PRESS OF KENTUCKY

Copyright © 1989 by The University Press of Kentucky
Scholarly publisher for the Commonwealth,
serving Bellarmine College, Berea College, Centre
College of Kentucky, Eastern Kentucky University,
The Filson Club, Georgetown College, Kentucky
Historical Society, Kentucky State University,
Morehead State University, Murray State University,
Northern Kentucky University, Transylvania University,
University of Kentucky, University of Louisville,
and Western Kentucky University.
Editorial and Sales Offices: Lexington, Kentucky 40506-0336

Library of Congress Cataloging-in-Publication Data

Nolan, Janet.
    Ourselves alone: women's emigration from Ireland, 1885-1920 /
Janet A. Nolan.
        p.   cm.
    Bibliography: p.
    Includes index.
    ISBN 0-8131-1684-8 (alk. paper)
    1. Young women—Ireland—Social conditions. 2. Single women—
Ireland—Social conditions. 3. Ireland—Emigration and
immigration—History. 4. Women immigrants—United States—History.
5. Irish—United States—History. I. Title. II. Title: Women's
emigration from Ireland, 1885-1920.
HQ1600.3.N65   1989   89-35145
304.8'3730415—dc20   CIP

To my grandmother,
Mary Ann Donovan Nolan
and her son,
William Francis Nolan

Contents

Tables

Figures

Acknowledgments

My greatest debt is to my teacher and advisor, Professor Emeritus Emiliana P. Noether of the University of Connecticut. Without her encouragement and expertise, this work might never have been completed. Warm thanks are also due to Professors Bruce M. Stave and Irene Q. Brown of the University of Connecticut, Gary Thurston of the University of Rhode Island, and Larry McCaffrey of Loyola University of Chicago for their thoughtful reading and substantive comments.

The completion of this study was also made possible by the generous financial support of both the University of Connecticut's Research Foundation and Loyola University of Chicago's Faculty Development Stipend. In addition, I owe special thanks to Robert Vrecenak and his staff in the Interlibrary Loan Department at the University of Connecticut, Richard Coughlin of the O'Neill Library at Boston College, and the staffs of the National Library of Ireland in Dublin, the Newberry Library in Chicago, and the Cudahy Library at Loyola University of Chicago. Professor Ruth-Ann Harris of Northeastern University has also been more than generous in sharing with me the fruits of her imaginative and productive scholarship.

I wish to express my appreciation and thanks to my friends and family, including my aunt Helen and cousin John Donovan, who lent me their memories, and my aunt-by-marriage Margaret Nolan, who, like her mother-in-law Mary Ann Donovan, left Ireland alone. My gratitude also extends to Susan Rogers and Sylvia Rdzak for their patience and good humor during the several typings of this manuscript, and to Professor Lew Erenberg of Loyola University of Chicago for freeing me forever from the tyranny of correction fluid.

Although all these teachers, family, and friends have helped me hone my ideas over the evolution of this work, I take full responsibility for its content, as well as for any errors it might contain.

Chicago, 1989

OURSELVES ALONE

Introduction:
Going Alone

In early April 1888, sixteen-year-old Mary Ann Donovan stood alone on the quays of Queenstown in County Cork waiting to board a ship bound for Boston in far-off America. Her parents had died a few months before, making Mary Ann and her brother John the only members of the family remaining in Ireland. Older sister Ellen had already gone to America. Her letters home were bright spots in the Donovan household in Skibbereen and were eagerly read when the "man with the letters from Bandon" made his weekly trip to the town. After their parents' deaths, Ellen sent the passage money so that her sister could join her.

Mary Ann looked about her. From where she stood, she could read the name, S. S. *Marathon,* in foot-high letters that stretched along the bow of the ship that would be her home as she crossed the water. It had been a two-day trip from Skibbereen to Queenstown and the ship. Brother John had driven her by cart to Bandon. From there, she had boarded a train to Cork city and, eventually, to the port. John stayed behind. He planned to sell the family farm, and then he too would join his sisters.

As the restraining ropes were lowered, the crowd on the docks surged forward, pushing Mary Ann toward America, along with thousands of other young farm girls like her, toward a better life in a new land.

This was to be the last voyage of the *Marathon.* After a troubled crossing, the vessel broke down in a northeast gale, one day's journey out of Boston Harbor. Towed to the city, never to sail again, the ship carried Mary Ann to America nonetheless.

Table 1. Percentage by Sex among Immigrants to the United States, Selected National Groups, 1899-1910

Nationality	% Male	% Female
Irish	48	52
Other British Isles	64	37
Scandinavian	62	38
Jewish	57	43
Italian	79	21

Source: Census for the United States, Table 12, in U.S. Congress, Senate, *Reports of the Immigration Commission: Statistical Review of Immigration, 1820-1910; Distribution of Immigrants 1850-1900,* 61st Cong., 3d sess., 1911, S. Doc. 756, p. 47.

In her adopted land she married and gave birth to nine children, one of whom became my father.

Mary Ann Donovan was one of almost 700,000 young, usually unmarried women, traveling alone, who composed most of the emigrants leaving Ireland between 1885 and 1920.[1] This large, sustained migration of single women is an anomaly in the history of European emigration: except for the Irish, only Swedish women emigrated independently from their families in significant numbers. But young, unmarried women were the majority among Swedish emigrants for only five years, between 1894 and 1899,[2] whereas single women dominated Irish emigration for thirty-five years. By the first decade of the twentieth century, the female majority among Irish emigrants was unique among Europeans once again, as can be seen in table 1, which gives immigration totals for the United States, the most popular immigrant destination in the late nineteenth and the early twentieth centuries.

The women who left Ireland during this period did so because they had grown ever more superfluous in their home communities as new demographic and economic patterns transformed Irish life in the half-century before 1880. These changes had lessened these women's chances for becoming wives and thereby attaining adult social and economic status. Since no corresponding expansion of new biological, economic, or social opportunities for unmarried women had taken place, the position of women deteriorated despite a rise in overall economic prosperity. Rather than accept their newly marginal lives as celibate dependents on family farms, however, more and more women left Ireland. By the 1880s their emigration reached epidemic-like proportions, especially in the west and the southwest, the regions undergoing the most abrupt changes in population and economic organization. In view of Irish women's increasingly restricted lives, their decision to emigrate becomes a remarkable example of female self-determination.

Nevertheless, the accepted interpretations of both Irish and overall European emigration have neither isolated nor examined the implications of the departure of large numbers of women from Ireland. In fact, most studies of emigration, if they mention women at all, see them as passive rather than active participants in the migration process. For instance, Oscar Handlin saw emigration as an uprooting experience that caused alienation from the original culture, in social as well as geographical terms.[3] While others disagree that emigration caused cultural breakdown, they emphasize the importance of the traditional family in female emigration. In their studies of southern Italian women, Rudolph Vecoli and Virginia Yans-McLaughlin have each demonstrated that these women emigrated as part of a family migration and served as carriers of traditional culture abroad; migration did not alter the woman's role as wife within the family economy.[4] A similar pattern has been found among eastern European Jewish female emigrants: they too traveled as family members, maintaining their Old World status.[5]

Valuable as these insights into the process of female emigration are, they do not apply to the almost 700,000 mostly unmarried women leaving Ireland between 1885 and 1920. As single women, these emigrants had no wifely role within a family economy.[6] Their emigration did not represent a family's migration, nor did they serve as carriers abroad of an intact traditional culture as did their Italian or Jewish contemporaries.

Clearly, there was an extra dimension to Irish women's decision to emigrate during this period. Their motivation for leaving their homes needs to be identified, for until this discrete period in both Irish and overall European emigration history is understood, our knowledge of women's role in shaping emigration patterns remains incomplete.

Several factors have contributed to the lack of knowledge about female emigration from Ireland in the late nineteenth and early twentieth centuries. First, despite the availability of numerical data documenting the existence of this unusual generation, only recently have historians started to look at the history of women as such, thereby asking new questions of historical data already at hand. In addition, until the last few decades, as the study of earlier societies "from the bottom up" has come into vogue, few scholars showed much interest in the lives and expectations of the common man, let alone the common woman.

Second, gathering data on Irish social history is particularly difficult, for several reasons. Revolution in Ireland in the early twentieth century interrupted official record keeping and contributed to the destruction of existing archival material. Most of the documents stored in the Public Record Office in Dublin, for example, were destroyed in the fighting there in 1922. As a result, important sources for the writing of Irish social history have been forever lost, including much of the material gathered in the censuses between 1813 and 1851. Further, the manuscript censuses for 1861 through 1891 were never preserved.

Third, government funding in the Republic of Ireland for the surveying and cataloguing of local archival material of interest to social historians has also been very limited. Although a manuscript commission was instituted in 1929, the scope of archival retrieval in the Republic remains narrow and so far has concentrated on the legal and business papers of estate owners. Useful as these documents are, few papers outside this category have been located or centralized.[7]

Since much of the material pertaining to the social and economic activities of the Irish in the nineteenth and early twentieth centuries remains scattered or lost, the official documents that have survived, especially census and emigration reports, are among the best sources available for the study of female emigration. But even these documents have their limitations. For instance, although attempts to count the Irish were made throughout the early nineteenth century (and even earlier), they depended on tax collectors' records and oral responses from reluctant taxpayers. They are unscientific and unreliable as a result.[8]

With the censuses of 1841, the year of the first complete census, and 1851, the year when emigration statistics first appear in the census, we have firmer numerical evidence about the nature of Irish life. In addition, the number of those still speaking the Irish language—an important indicator of the extent of traditional ways of life—was also listed in the census in 1851. In 1861 religious affiliation was added, and in 1864 the registration of births, marriages, and deaths became compulsory. In 1876 the separate publication of annual government statistics on emigration began. Although 1920 marks the last year of a single census and emigration report for all of Ireland, separate reports for the Free State and Northern Ireland were introduced in 1926.[9]

Despite the existence of official data on the demographics of Irish life over the last century and a half, the study of Irish social history remains incomplete. Since it is concerned with the lives of those least likely to record their experiences, social history must depend on quantitative evidence when qualitative documentation is not available.[10] Nevertheless, unofficial papers— especially emigrant letters—as Arnold Schrier has shown, are another important source of information about the lives and aspirations of the Irish during the period to be discussed here.[11] Since we know that the "letter from America" was commonplace and that it served as an important means for keeping family members on both sides of the Atlantic in personal and financial communication, these emigrant letters are an invaluable source.

Although these documents have had an even worse survival rate than have the more public records, two recent studies have been based on them. The first, by Kerby Miller, illustrates nineteenth-century attitudes toward emigration by using evidence found in emigrant letters and other contemporary reports in collections located in Canada, Great Britain, Northern Ireland, the Republic of Ireland, and throughout the United States.[12] The second, by Ruth-Ann Harris, analyzes 4,930 classified advertisements placed in the Boston *Pilot* between 1831 and 1916 by emigrants seeking relatives or friends already in the United States.[13] Each of these studies takes an innovative approach to discovering the human dimension of emigration from nineteenth- and early twentieth-century Ireland. Nonetheless, as one scholar of Irish emigration has noted, no complete guide to Irish emigrant letters yet exists.[14]

The study of women in Irish society presents an even greater challenge than does that of their emigration. Until very recently, study of the social history of Ireland (like that of other countries) was based on the assumption that the female experience, if acknowledged at all, reflected that of males.[15] For example, although the commercialization of the Irish economy over the course of the nineteenth century has received much scholarly attention, little work exists on the impact of this change on women.[16] Although Conrad Arensberg and Solon Kimball's seminal investigation of early twentieth century rural life offers important insight into traditional rural mores, emphasis is placed on the male experience, as it is in subsequent studies done by others.[17] Women are seen as passive outsiders in male culture and not as equally active shapers of Irish life.

More recently, new approaches to the Irish past have sought to correct this scholarly oversight of women's impact on social change. Hasia Diner's work on Irish female immigrants in the United States[18] and Pauline Jackson's discussion of the causes of female emigration in the post-Famine period[19] are two recent examples. Lynn Hollen Lees's study of the Irish in London in the immediate post-Famine period,[20] Robert Kennedy's investigation of Irish women's lives in the late nineteenth and early twentieth centuries,[21] and each of the essays in Margaret Mac-Curtain and Donncha O'Corrain's collection[22] also focus on women in Irish history. Valuable as these studies are, though, they raise as many questions as they answer about female emigration from Ireland between 1885 and 1920.

As a result, this book fills an important gap. While Ireland was struggling for independence from British control in the late nineteenth and early twentieth centuries, Irish women were seeking a separate independence from their increasingly marginal positions in post-Famine society. Consequently, the migration of this generation of young unmarried women represents not only the culmination of nineteenth century Irish emigration but also a new direction in European female emigration as a whole.

An understanding of this phenomenon can be gained by asking new questions of the data found in census and emigration reports and by providing a new framework for interpreting Irish social, economic, and even political history during this period. The statistical evidence documenting the mass migration of unmarried women from Ireland between 1885 and 1920 has been available for the better part of the century; and the informal family histories of many of the Irish living in the United States today contain at least one mother, grandmother, aunt, or sister who emigrated alone from Ireland in the thirty-five years after 1885;[23] but curiously, few scholars have noted the existence of this anomalous emigrant group or assessed its impact on Irish history.

This study, then, is concerned with asking new questions of the raw numerical data gathered from Irish and American census and emigration reports, as well as of the more literary evidence found in emigrant letters and oral histories. Often, like the proverbial picture, numbers speak more loudly than words, and so tables derived from the data in government documents are interspersed throughout the text. These tables serve not only to advance arguments made within the text itself, but also to provide a more vivid picture of the nature of Irish emigration than words alone could do.

By rethinking the accepted interpretations of Irish social, economic, and emigration history, we can solve the puzzle of female emigration from Ireland between 1885 and 1920. Chapter 1 discusses the demographic and economic changes that transformed Ireland in the fifty years before 1880. Chapter 2 assesses the impact of these changes on the lives of women. Chapter 3 traces the history of emigration from Ireland, showing how the combined forces of demographic and economic change led to the loss of entire segments of the Irish population, including, after 1880, its young women. Chapter 4 examines the connection between the mass migration of young women from Ireland and the demographic and economic stagnation of Irish life. Chapter 5 addresses the relationship between the lives of women in Ireland and their lives after emigration. Finally, the conclusion evaluates the reasons for the mass exodus of these young, unmarried Irish women during this period.

Together, these chapters demonstrate that the role of women in social change is not as derivative as has been commonly assumed, at least in the case of Irish women.[24] The emigration of this generation did not represent a rejection of traditional female roles, nor did it mean a passive transferral abroad of intact female roles. Instead, these women emigrated so that they could actively recover their lost importance in Irish life. Since their home communities could no longer accommodate their aspirations, these young women chose to pursue their goals abroad.

Mary Ann Donovan died in 1960 at the age of eighty-eight, thirty years after the death of her husband and seventy-two years after her arrival in the United States. Like her sisters who also emigrated from Ireland during those years, she found fulfillment in her new country by returning to traditional patterns of female life while simultaneously embracing the new opportunities of urban America. As a wage earner, wife, mother, and community activist, she was able to attain traditional female status, a status no longer available to women in Ireland. But Mary Ann Donovan was not an isolated case. Her journey from Skibbereen to New England is representative of thousands of other journeys made by her contemporaries, who could truly claim that they had seized control over their lives, by themselves, alone.

CHAPTER ONE

The Changing Face of Ireland 1830-1880

The story of late nineteenth- and early twentieth-century female emigration from Ireland begins in the half century before 1880. In the course of those fifty years, the country was in a state of flux, as overpopulation and periodic famine forced people to alter their way of life. Between 1830 and 1880, depopulation replaced overpopulation, and land consolidation and market agriculture replaced land subdivision and subsistence tillage, first in the north and the east, then in the south, and, finally, in the west. Despite these changes, in 1880 Ireland still depended on population decline to maintain an economy based on agriculture rather than industry. Emigration was responsible for much of this decline.

The changing demographic and economic conditions in Ireland during the course of the nineteenth century reflect the incomplete modernization of this British colony on the periphery of western Europe. Like its counterparts in the region, Ireland underwent an agricultural revolution in the eighteenth century when the potato was introduced as the subsistence crop of the island. By the early nineteenth century, although poverty was ubiquitous, the Irish were taller and heavier than their counterparts elsewhere in western Europe.[1]

Contemporaries remarked on their robust health, and historians have noted that the average Irish person, male or female, although confined to a potato diet, was extremely well nourished.[2] "Let [the] ignorant . . . who say that potatoes and milk is not nourishing food, look at the children, generally in rags, but with every appearance and reality of ruddy health," admonished one such informant touring Ireland in the early nineteenth century, ". . . [or] let them attend a football or hurling

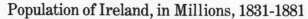

Population of Ireland, in Millions, 1831-1881

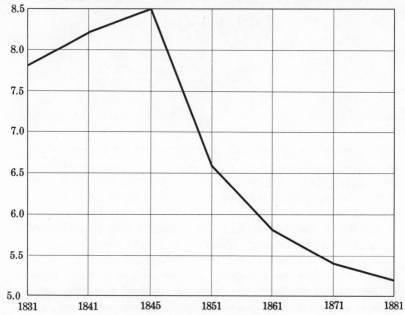

Source: Census of Ireland, in <u>Irish Historical Statistics,</u> table 3, p.3.

match, and see the superiority of potatoes and milk over . . .
cheese and . . . beer—the young men performing feats of activity
that would astonish a bread-and-cheese Englishman."[3]

As a result of the healthful spread of potato cultivation after
1750, the Irish population increased at the highest rate in the
British Isles, doubling from 4.4 million to 8.5 million between
1788 and 1845.[4] After 1850, however, while the population elsewhere in western Europe continued growing, that of Ireland fell.
By 1881 fewer people lived in the country than had in 1831.

Throughout western Europe, the population increases that
began in the eighteenth century contributed to subsequent
revolutions in agriculture, industry, and political organization.
These changes, in turn, provided new means of support and
accommodation for continuing population growth. In England,

the agricultural revolution and subsequent population increase were followed by widespread changes in the economy. By the early nineteenth century, as England's population began to rise at an unprecedented rate, industrialization absorbed this new human surplus. Little such economic development took place in Ireland, however, where the economy remained primarily agricultural and preindustrial.

Since Britain needed a market, not competition, for its burgeoning industries, its polices favored British enterprise rather than Irish. In addition, Ireland lacked some of the natural resources, the capital, and the entrepreneurial class needed for an industrial revolution. As a result, Irish agricultural, industrial, and political systems remained static despite dramatic demographic change.[5] Without new economic resources to support the population increase, ever larger numbers of Irish faced a future of diminishing economic returns. Nevertheless, although contemporaries remarked on the widespread poverty of the Irish in the first half of the nineteenth century, as long as potatoes could be grown, population increase could be sustained. By the turn of the nineteenth century, Malthusian restraints on population growth in Ireland had disappeared.

These changes affected women in two major ways. First, most could marry and reproduce because potato cultivation allowed the establishment of new households in the subsistence economy. Second, because women held an important demographic and economic position in the labor-intensive economy of pre-Famine Ireland, they exercised a high degree of autonomy over their choice of when and whom to marry. As coproducers within the subsistence family economy, wives enjoyed a high status in rural Irish life.

After 1830, and especially after the devastating famine of the late 1840s, however, unchecked population growth and reliance on subsistence potato cultivation had mostly disappeared in the north and the east. The Famine was only a partial check to the demographic and economic patterns that had emerged after 1780, nonetheless. Although the Famine marked the end to overall population growth, patterns of early and universal marriage and reliance on subsistence tillage persisted among the much depleted laboring class, especially in the west and south-

west, into the 1880s. High marital fertility also remained un-
curbed among all population groups throughout the country.

Consequently, although the trauma of the Famine signaled
the end of population increase in most areas of Ireland, other
factors also contributed to the falling population levels after
1845. Since industrialization and land redistribution did not
occur after the Famine, the Irish economy remained pre-
cariously perched on an archaic agricultural system. As a result, the rural majority soon demonstrated new demographic
and economic behaviors. These new ways of life lowered the
birthrate by delaying and restricting marriage, and reduced the
number of people who could be supported by agriculture by
changing the patterns of land use. Although Ireland eventually
recovered from the worst ravages of overpopulation and mass
starvation, renewed economic well-being came about only at the
price of continuing depopulation and persistent emigration. As
a result, increasing numbers of Irish women lost their reproductive as well as their productive roles in the third quarter of the
nineteenth century.

The mass migration of women from Ireland in the course of
the late nineteenth and early twentieth centuries, therefore,
reflected the simultaneous impact of the new demographic and
economic patterns of post-Famine Ireland and the loss of the
older but equally innovative patterns of Irish female life that
had appeared in the late eighteenth century.

Changing marriage patterns in the half century before 1830 had
a direct impact on population levels in those years. Beginning in
the late eighteenth century, as the population rose with the
spread of potato cultivation, most Irish men and women con-
formed to the European custom of marrying in their mid-
twenties.[6] As one early nineteenth-century observer wrote, "An
unmarried man . . . or a woman . . . is rarely to be met in the
country parts."[7] Although the average age of marriage partners
slowly increased after 1830, especially among land-holding tenant farmers, more Irish married and at younger ages before the
Famine than they ever would again.

The decade following 1841 saw a rapid rise in the age at which most Irish would marry as economic disaster forced agricultural laborers to adopt the marital behavior of the better-off farming classes in order to survive. This trend continued throughout the late nineteenth century, and into the twentieth. By the 1880s the Irish married at the latest ages in Europe, over age thirty-four for men and over age twenty-nine for women.[8]

The marriage rate decreased as the marriage age increased.While at least three quarters of the Irish married before the Famine, by 1881 only one-third of their descendants were husbands or wives.[9] Although the west was the last region to abandon pre-Famine demographic and economic behavior, by the 1870s marriage rates had decreased even there. For instance, while slightly more than ten marriages for each one thousand in the population of Knockainy Parish in County Limerick took place in 1840, fewer than half that number occurred in the parish in 1880.[10]

Changing marriage patterns in turn affected population levels. Since most women married at relatively young ages before the Famine, and because fertility rises with the length of marriage if birth control is not used, population increase among the mostly Catholic agricultural majority was inevitable. Although population statistics are unreliable before 1851, one trustworthy estimate places the birthrate at 33-40 per 1,000 in the population in 1841, the highest rate in the British Isles.[11] Another indication of the high rates of population increase in pre-Famine Ireland is the high number of people living in the average Irish household. Though households were smaller among the poorer laborers than among the richer farmers, who often kept servants, the average pre-Famine Irish household, which usually contained a nuclear family, held five or six individuals, larger by one than its English counterpart. In the west, the region with the highest birth rate before the Famine, six or more individuals lived together in each typical household.[12]

After the Famine, the trend toward delayed and restricted marriage played an equally important role in the rapid and persistent decline in population. As marriage rates fell and as the age of marriage rose in the half century after 1830, fewer and fewer children were born over time. In 1864, the first year of the civil registration of births, 136,414 children were born. In 1880 only 128,086 births were recorded. By that year the birthrate had fallen to 24.7 for each 1,000 in the population.[13]

Once again the birthrates in Knockainy Parish, like those in Inishkillane Parish in County Clare, mirrored the countrywide pattern. In Knockainy, 37.3 births per 1,000 in the population occurred in 1830. By 1880 only 22 births per 1,000 in the population were entered into parish records. In 1843, 209 baptisms were performed in Inishkillane. By 1893 only 63 took place. Although marital fertility remained stable throughout the period, the low numbers of marriages in these parishes offset any potential population growth.[14]

Throughout the half century after 1830, changing population levels reflected the economic well-being of the Irish. As the population rose in the first half of the nineteenth century, the standard of living worsened. Conversely, as the population fell after 1845, the lives of the still agricultural population gradually improved. Confined to a finite amount of land, the Irish limited their numbers to promote economic recovery. By the late nineteenth century, population growth and subsistence tillage had ended almost everywhere in Ireland. These changes, in turn, would have a dramatic impact on the position of women in rural Ireland, as we shall see.

"Nothing can be more *extreme* than the poverty of the peasant," exclaimed one traveler in Ireland in 1844,[15] echoing the general view of his contemporaries that Ireland on the eve of the Famine was one of Europe's most undeveloped areas. Irish agriculture and manufacturing had not always been on the brink of disaster, however. At the turn of the century, few Irish had lived at the subsistence level. Rents were paid in cash earned from domestic textile production, dairying, and poultry and egg sales—activities dominated by women. But the end of the Napoleonic Wars in 1815 and the rescission of the laws protecting Irish manufacturing in the late 1820s allowed British goods to flood Irish markets, causing a fall in demand for both Irish products and labor.[16] Furthermore, as population growth outstripped that of available resources, Irish home manufacturing simultaneously succumbed to mechanized British competition. As supplementary sources of cash income disappeared, more and more Irish were forced to depend on subsistence agriculture alone for their survival.

The greatest population growth before the Famine was recorded in areas least able to support it. While the total population in Ireland rose by 20 percent between 1821 and 1841, the population of the west, the region hardest hit by agricultural depression and the contraction of cottage industry, increased by 30 percent in the same two decades. In areas of Sligo, Kerry, and Leitrim, population increases of 40 percent occurred between 1821 and 1841.[17] Moreover, the proportion of landless laborers and their families increased in the overall population in those years. In 1821 only between one-quarter and one-third of the population had been subsistence laborers and their families. By 1841 over one-half of all adult males lived on the subsistence level, and over 40 percent of the remaining population were dependents under age fifteen or over age sixty-five.[18] The observation that "the only solace these miserable mortals have . . . is in matrimony; accordingly, they all marry young,"[19] made in the late eighteenth century, continued to describe the marital behavior of the poorest groups among the Irish well into the nineteenth century.

As the number of people dependent on subsistence potato cultivation climbed, the fragmentation of land into ever smaller holdings kept pace. Since each child in a family was given part of his or her parents' holding upon marriage, the average size of land holdings decreased with each new and larger generation. By 1841 over 80 percent of all land holdings in Ireland covered less than fifteen acres and fully 45 percent of all tenant-held farms averaged less than five acres in size. The number of holdings smaller than one acre also increased, especially in the overpopulated west. For instance, in 1841, on the Gweedore Estate in Donegal, more than twenty-six people lived on a land subdivision only one-half acre in size.[20] On the eve of the Famine, over four-fifths of the Irish subsisted on densely populated, impoverished holdings.

Another measurement of the restructuring of Irish landholdings before the Famine is found in the diminishing area of pasture reserved for livestock. As subsistence potato cultivation and land subdivision spread before 1845, the quarter acre of land allotted to each cow for pasture decreased accordingly. This measurement, once called a "cow's grass," now became a "cow's foot." By the end of the pre-Famine period, each grazing animal was given a "cow's toe" for pasture, an area only one eighth the size of the "cow's grass." [21]

Overall, the number of people per square mile of arable land in Ireland rose from 316 to 381 between 1821 and 1841. These increases were highest in the west and lowest in the east, reflecting the geographical differences in demographic trends. By 1841, while an average of 411 people in Connaught and 396 people in Munster lived on each square mile of arable land, only 281 people lived on each square mile of farmland in Leinster. In Ulster, where domestic industry persisted and industrialization did occur, population densities before the Famine remained the highest in Ireland—reaching 434 people per square mile of arable land in 1841. Since the landless in the north were able to find alternative means of support in the heavily cash-oriented economy of that province, however, population densities in Ulster were less ominous on the eve of the Famine than they were in the west and the southwest. [22]

The system of land tenancy also contributed to the fragmentation of land holdings and to the increasing poverty of the rural Irish before 1845. Until the advent of government reform in the late nineteenth century, landlords, usually absentee, owned 80 percent of the land in Ireland. Outside of Ulster, where tenants had more control over their holdings, leases were oral and were renegotiated annually. Leases were not inheritable, and a tenant rented only the land: he owned neither his house nor any capital improvement he might make on his holding. Since the landlord could raise the rent if a tenant improved his holding and evict him if he did not pay the higher rent, [23] a tenant lacked the incentive to improve his holding or limit his reproduction.

Nevertheless, as long as rents were paid, landlords had little interest in how the land was used or in the number of people living on it. As a result, in order to maximize their profits in overpopulated Ireland, tenant farmers subdivided their holdings among the growing number of landless laborers. In general, the landless exchanged labor for housing (usually a hovel with mud floors and walls) and a small plot for planting po-

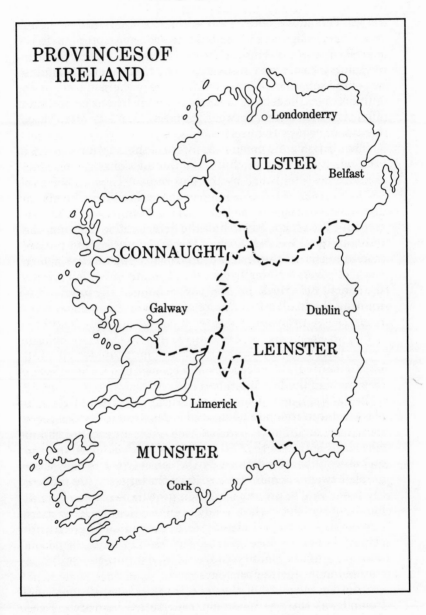

tatoes. This subsistence rental, or conacre, was leased for eleven-month periods, and as land became ever more precious in the course of the pre-Famine years, these rentals became increasingly costly and insecure.[24] On the eve of the Famine, when the subsistence crop would fail everywhere in Ireland, the gulf between the tenant farmers and their tenant laborers was almost as wide as that between the farmers and the often absentee estate owners themselves.[25]

The British government was aware of the growing poverty in Ireland. By one count, fully 114 commissions and 60 select committees established by the government between 1800 and 1833 investigated the growing economic crisis there.[26] As late as 1845, the government-sponsored Devon Commission fruitlessly continued to seek a way to halt the deterioration of living standards in rural Ireland. Each of these committees and commissions agreed that the system of land ownership was the primary cause of poverty. Nevertheless, the strength of British belief in the sanctity of private property overwhelmed any proposals for limiting the landlord's absolute control over his land, and as a result, no government-sponsored land reforms were instituted. Rather, a Poor Law for Ireland was enacted in 1838, creating workhouses for the growing number of destitute forced off the land as agricultural depression deepened under the effects of free trade in the late 1830s and early 1840s.

In addition, few if any of the rural unemployed could be absorbed into Ireland's towns and cities. Outside of Belfast, no industrial or urban expansion took place in the pre-Famine period. In 1841, less than 20 percent of the Irish lived in towns and cities, liberally defined by the census, to this day, as any group of twenty or more houses. Even the largest cities reflected the lower rate of urban population growth before the Famine. Furthermore, those who already lived in cities also faced unemployment as cottage industry disappeared and agricultural prices fell. For instance, in 1841 over one-quarter of the population of Ennis in County Clare depended directly on potato cultivation for their subsistence.[27]

Another measure of the increasing poverty in post-1830 Ireland was the rise in seasonal migration in search of cash wages overseas. By 1841 an estimated sixty thousand Irish annually traveled to Britain for part of the year to earn money to pay rents on their holdings at home.[28] As long as the subsistence standard of living could be ensured by further land subdivision, increased reliance on the potato, and seasonal migration, population growth could continue despite a contracting economy.

By the end of the pre-Famine period, then, fully half of all the potatoes produced each year in Ireland were directly consumed by their producers.[29] The advent of the potato blight in 1845, however, meant that even the limited pre-Famine diet of potatoes and an occasional fish became unavailable to millions of Irish. From that point forward, subsistence agriculture and population growth were no longer compatible.

In the three decades between 1850 and 1880, economic reorganization became not only imperative but, more important, possible. Population decrease and the reintroduction of cash-producing agriculture led to gradually improving living conditions for those who remained on the land. Ultimately, a cash economy based on land consolidation and market agriculture replaced the subsistence economy of the pre-Famine period. In contrast to the steady economic decline of the pre-Famine period, post-Famine Ireland enjoyed slow economic improvement. By 1880 these changes had reached even the remote west.

The economic recovery of the post-Famine period did not benefit all groups in rural Ireland equally. Since the land system remained intact for most of the period, prosperity depended on depopulation rather than on innovation in agriculture or industry. As a result, although post-Famine society was rife with change, the fundamental Irish problem of creating an economy that could support all of the population remained unsolved.

Nevertheless, as population decrease eased pressure on the land, survivors of the Famine developed a new outlook about their economic well-being. No longer satisfied with the precarious existence endured by their pre-Famine forebears, those who remained on the land consciously sought to improve their material status. As one chronicler of rural life noted, "it had passed into an article of religion . . . that the whole business of life was to succeed, no matter by what means."[30]

The new material aspirations that arose from the renewal of agricultural prosperity after the Famine were reflected in changing marriage and inheritance patterns among the rural population. By the 1850s, the inheritance of the family farm by only one son and the dowering of only one daughter, neither necessarily the eldest siblings in a family, had become the norm, except in the west.[31] Since siblings no longer shared equally in their parents' property, marriage became increasingly delayed, as brothers and sisters jockeyed for position, and restricted, as land consolidation increased. By the end of the post-Famine period, marriage was an economic institution, arranged by a professional matchmaker and designed to ensure the preservation and the improvement of a family's economic well-being.

As marriage evolved into an economic institution above all else, a man married not when he wanted a wife but when his farm needed a woman, and romantic love was increasingly scorned by both participants in and observers of the marriage ritual. According to post-Famine peasant lore, "a good, hard-working stump of a girl" was what was needed in a wife, and in Kerry everyone knew that "good looks don't boil the pot."[32] In choosing a wife, grooms were advised to "take the girl with two cows [for a dowry]. There isn't a difference of a cow . . . between any two women in the world."[33] Anti-female sentiments like these became so pervasive in Irish society after the Famine that farmers were not the only upwardly mobile group to seek economic gain rather than romance when they married: shopkeepers too were warned that they "must get a wife who can help . . . in the shop."[34]

These changing marriage and inheritance patterns fostered a steady increase in the size of individual land holdings after the Famine. In 1841 the median size of all farms larger than 1 acre had only been 10.8 acres. By 1851, 15.6 acres was the norm. By 1876, 18.5 acres was the median size of all holdings larger than 1 acre.[35] In addition, the percentage of holdings over 30 acres in size more than quadrupled between 1841 and 1881, rising from 7 to 31 percent of the total number of farms.[36]

The new economic prosperity and materialistic outlook in post-Famine Ireland can also be measured in terms of improved rural housing and increased rural cash reserves after the Famine. In 1841, almost one half of the total population, and fully 90 percent of the population in Connaught, lived in one-room, windowless cabins, the lowest category of housing counted by the Census. By 1881, however, one half of the rural Irish were living in improved housing, according to the census, and even in Connaught only 68 percent of the inhabitants continued to call one-room hovels home.[37] Bank deposits held by farmers also rose after the Famine. Farmers' cash reserves in Irish banks doubled from £8 million to £16 million in the 1850s, and by 1876 farmers had deposited £33 million in Irish banks. Besides saving his growing cash surplus, the Irish farmer also began to spend more of his income on retail goods. His diet grew more diversified as the level of per capita retail purchases of food rose.[38] Other formerly luxury goods also became more common: by the end of the 1870s, per capita tobacco consumption in Ireland matched that of Britain.[39]

But the post-Famine economic revival was not based on any industrial growth or expansion of manufacturing. In fact, these sectors of the economy actually shrank in the thirty years after 1850, and most Irish cities did not grow. Although the overall population of towns rose from 1.1 million in 1851 to 1.9 million in 1881, this growth was concentrated in the larger cities, especially Belfast. Elsewhere, town populations either stagnated or fell during the post-Famine period, especially those in the west.[40]

Depopulation also inhibited industrial and urban growth in the late nineteenth and early twentieth centuries. The expansion of Belfast from a preindustrial market town of 19,000 people in 1800 to a major industrial city with a population of 100,000 in 1851 was a singular phenomenon in Ireland, and even there, industry contracted in the last half of the nineteenth century. Further, although there was some growth in the populations of Derry and Dublin after 1850, neither city expanded industrially.

Elsewhere, while the development of new railroad lines meant that the better-situated towns could become important wholesale and retail centers for the surrounding countryside, better communications with the outside world were a mixed blessing if the well-being of all Irish towns is taken into consideration. The coming of the railroad did create a commercial revolution in some towns, but it also helped bring about a decline in the profitability of local crafts because it eased the introduction of cheap British manufactured goods into local markets. Moreover, railroads enabled rural people to quit their farms easily, travel to seaports, and leave the country.[41] The railroads, therefore, both increased supply and decreased demand for manufactured goods in town shops. As a result, town population fell, and Irish industry actually disappeared in Galway, Cork, and Limerick after the Famine.[42]

The demise of small industry in Ireland was rapid enough to be noticeable to the rural population. As one man remembered, "Within . . . ten miles of the nearest town [to my birthplace], . . . [there were] small industries. A sugar factory in Mallow, . . . a chocolate factory, . . . and flour mills . . . but [they] disappeared, . . . went out of business . . . the ruins of the buildings were still there, and at one time, I believe, [they] employed quite a few people."[43]

Despite the growing cash incomes in rural areas after the Famine, therefore, mass consumption of Irish-made goods did not occur. As one woman whose father had emigrated remembered, her father's family's purchase of a thirty-seven-acre farm in County Clare in 1862 meant "they had everything . . enough to eat . . . their own butter, eggs, pigs, meat . . . enough peat for heating purposes . . . [and] they sold some of the [excess]."[44] Such self-sufficient prosperity severely limited any potential demand for store-bought food and other commodities. And finally, in the forty years after 1841 rural areas lost one half their population. Depopulation, even more than lack of demand, limited or prevented the expansion of Irish industry and towns in the last half of the nineteenth century.

Nevertheless, despite the lack of urban or industrial growth and of any true revolution in agricultural techniques, the overall economy did become more prosperous after 1850. Ironically, the very decrease in population levels that had helped retard urban and industrial expansion was the single most important factor in the increasing prosperity of rural Ireland in the third quarter of the nineteenth century. Without steady population

Table 2: Population Change and Emigration, Ireland,
1780-1880

Year	Population	Years	Emigration	Population Change
1788	4,389,000	1780-1845	1,750,000[a]	—
1845	8,500,000	1845-1850	1,000,000[a]	+ 4,111,000
1851	6,552,385	1851-1860	1,136,116	− 1,947,615
1861	5,798,967	1861-1870	771,900	− 753,418
1871	5,412,377	1871-1880	618,503	− 386,590
1881	5,174,836	—	—	− 237,541

Source: L.M. Cullen, *An Economic Hisotry of Ireland Since 1660* p. 134; and the census and emigration reports between 1851 and 1881 in *Irish Historical Statistics,* table 54, pp. 261-63.

[a]Estimated

decrease, the spread of land consolidation and cash-producing pasturage could not have happened.

The renewed economic well-being of farmers after the Famine came about at the price of dispossessing large numbers of agricultural laborers and their families. In fact, more than 5 million Irish emigrated between 1780 and 1880, and most of the people who left the country in those years had been forced off the land by demographic and economic change. By siphoning off newly superfluous groups within the population, emigration eased population pressure on the land and facilitated land consolidation and the reintroduction of market agriculture. As early as 1845, emigration began to have a major impact on population levels within the country. The land "can be divided," as one emigrant pointed out, "but, if you divide a farm and give it to two sons, neither is going to have a heck of a lot. So I began to realize that [I] would have to go somewhere."[45] Millions of his countrymen and countrywomen did likewise, as the figures in table 2 attest.

Large-scale emigration from Ireland began in the half century before the Famine. Although no official records of the exact number of emigrants before 1851 exist, reliable estimates indicate that between 1815 and 1845, at least 1.5 million people left the country.[46] In these years, the highest emigration rates appeared in Ulster in the north and Leinster in the east, the areas that had been the first to adopt the new patterns of delayed and restricted marriage and market agriculture and were the closest to major ports of embarkation.[47] Elsewhere, seasonal, rather than permanent, emigration was the norm.

In the ten years after 1845, the Famine decade, well over a million people permanently left the country. Most studies of Famine emigration agree that at least 1 million emigrated between 1845 and 1850, and two-thirds of a million left between 1851 and 1854.[48] Between 1845 and 1851 the population fell by 2 million. Starvation and famine-induced disease accounted for half of this decrease; emigration accounted for the rest of it.

Regional differences in emigration persisted during the Famine. Though the potato blight was devastating throughout the country, it was most lethal in areas with the heaviest dependence on potato subsistence. As a result, the west and the southwest sustained the heaviest mortality, while the eastern and north central regions experienced the heaviest emigration in the late 1840s.[49]

As new demographic and economic patterns spread to the south after 1851, however, emigration from Munster rose. By the mid-1850s, Munster had the highest number of emigrants of all four provinces. In addition, while the overall annual emigration rates after 1855 were lower than those of the Famine decade, they were still approximately twice those of the pre-Famine period.[50] The pattern of widespread emigration that had begun well before the Famine was maintained throughout the third quarter of the nineteenth century.

But in the west, the Famine was only a temporary demographic watershed. Although this region had the highest rate of population increase before the Famine and the greatest rate of population loss during the Famine, by 1851 it had recovered its demographic equilibrium. Thereafter, the west lost population at a much lower rate than did the rest of Ireland.[51] This anomalous pattern reflected the region's lag in adopting new marriage and inheritance practices. As long as most people in the west and the southwest continued to marry at relatively young ages, emigration could offset natural increase.

Therefore, while emigration continued to drain large numbers of people from Ireland throughout the post-Famine period, a different emigration pattern distinguished areas that had undergone demographic and economic change from those that had not. Consequently, emigration from the west was intermittent, rising only in the years of acute agricultural crisis in the early 1860s and again in the late 1870s. Nevertheless, although emigration rates in the west after the Famine were lower than those in the rest of rural Ireland, seasonal migration remained important in the region, rising to 100,000 persons annually by the mid-1860s.[52] After the near-famine of the late 1870s, however, permanent emigration and population decline, spurred by the introduction of commercial agriculture, marked the end of subsistence life everywhere in Ireland, even in the west.[53]

CHAPTER TWO

Women and Social Change 1830-1880

As new demographic and economic patterns transformed Ireland after 1830, women grew ever more superfluous in Irish life. This lower female status represents a radical break with the past. Although rural society had always been patriarchal, the patterns of early and universal marriage and of widespread female employment in the half century before 1830 had assured women an integrated adult role as wives and cobreadwinners within the family economy. After 1830, however, as fewer and fewer marriages took place and as sources of cash income for women disappeared, the position of the increasing numbers of unmarried women deteriorated despite overall economic recovery. By 1880 more and more of these newly dispossessed women lived as celibate dependents on family farms with little or no hope of marrying or earning wages for their labor.

In addition to new demographic and economic restrictions, women also faced increasingly strict social controls that kept them from realizing an independent adult status. As more and more women remained unmarried long after reaching adulthood, severe sexual and social prohibitions, reinforced by the growing influence of the Catholic church in rural communities, inhibited contact between the sexes, even that between husbands and wives and between siblings. Consequently, women experienced growing isolation not only from men but also from other women.

Despite their diminished opportunities, women, no less than men, acquired the new material aspirations that accompanied economic recovery in the post-Famine period. These rising expectations stemmed not only from the results of agricultural reorganization but also from other advances in Irish life. For one thing, beginning in the 1830s, and becoming countrywide in the 1850s, national schools expanded English-language literacy. For another, the introduction of the penny post in the 1840s brought periodicals, letters from relatives living abroad, and other sources of information about the outside world to formerly remote and self-contained communities, even those in the west. Improvements in transportation also had an impact on the world view of the rural Irish. As a result, an ever larger number of unmarried women in the population saw the widening gap between their new social aspirations and their social realities.

In the half century before 1830, most of the Irish lived in self-sufficient communities, virtually isolated from the outside world. Even as late as 1841, 95 percent of the population lived in the counties of their birth.[1] In this subsistence rural world, kinship ties wove a strong web of reciprocity. Extended families were responsible for providing care for the elderly, jobs and housing for their members in times of distress, and attendance at family rituals of marriage and death. Relatives also joined in harvesting, building projects, and seasonal celebrations at regular intervals throughout the year.[2]

The communal structure of village life stood opposed to individual ambition or entrepreneurial innovation. Kinship obligations strengthened the attitude that the individual should obey the community's demands for social and economic conformity. The upwardly mobile were scorned for abandoning their culture for that of an alien group, and cultural attitudes reinforced the acceptance of unchanging poverty.[3] In fact, the prohibition against rising above one's neighbors was strong enough to survive emigration. "When we could afford a washerwoman," recalled one Irish-American, "Mother insisted on hanging up the clothes so the neighbors wouldn't know she had help. And we got her a maid too, [Mother] kept the blinds down on the kitchen side of the house so the neighbors couldn't see."[4] Within this enclosed world where few expected to improve their standard of living (or hid the fact from their neighbors if they did), women enjoyed a high status as wives, mothers, and coproducers in the family economy.

Furthermore, despite the strictures against individualism,

most studies of pre-Famine life agree that men and women alike freely chose their own mates.[5] Popular culture emphasized the erotic and romantic nature of the marital bond. The Catholic church also promoted early and universal marriage as an alternative to sin. Consequently, the overwhelming majority of the population married and lived in single family households on ever smaller plots of land, surrounded by a neighborhood of their extended families.

Since women could marry at will, illegitimacy and adultery were rare. In addition, severe social sanctions existed against a "woman's failure in chastity," and the law decreed that "females should be . . . guardians of their own honour, and be responsible in their own persons for all deviations from virtue." Although the father of an illegitimate child was under no legal obligation to provide support, few men withstood the equally severe social opprobrium against any derelictions of duty on their part: most married their pregnant girlfriends. There could "not be a more disgraceful event" to the Irish than the birth of an illegitimate child, and men and women alike bore the burden of stern social disapproval if they strayed from the prescribed path of marriage before parenthood.[6]

Nevertheless, although contemporaries reported that females were "signally chaste" and that "there were no more innocent girls than the Irish," unwed mothers were not unusual among servants living in their employers' households. In fact, the "gentleman's miss" was a fairly common figure. Since an unmarried pregnant female had no place in family-centered rural life, however, these unfortunate prospective mothers often migrated to cities and often became prostitutes. Even more drastic measures were taken by those who remained at home. Although abortion was rare, infanticide and the abandonment of illegitimate children were more common.[7]

Although the Catholic church mirrored peasant attitudes against premarital sexual activity, practicality rather than morality kept the illegitimacy rate from ever becoming more than 6 percent of the total number of births before the Famine.[8] In addition, there were too few priests and churches and even fewer nuns in those years to monitor the behavior of the rural population. Thus, although over 80 percent of the population in 1831 was Catholic (and this percentage was even higher in the west), only between 30 and 60 percent of the total Catholic population (and between 20 and 40 percent of those in the west) regularly attended mass in 1834.[9] Consequently, peasant values remained based on the traditional needs of the agricultural community rather than on any abstract moral sanctions imposed by the church.

Since the pre-Famine family was based on the free attachment of romantic love, it was more democratic than authoritarian. Although husbands were the nominal heads of households, wives exercised considerable power within the family. Married women controlled the house, the garden, the animals, and the children. They outranked their mothers-in-law and other members of their husbands' families in the domestic hierarchy. They also retained strong ties with the families of their birth, and many kept their maiden names. While women often presented public faces of docility, they regularly challenged male authority at home. Domestic brawls were as common a theme as romantic attraction in popular lore.[10]

The democratic nature of the pre-Famine family also extended to relationships among siblings. Patriarchal patterns of male inheritance were not widespread in the early years of the century, and all children shared in the division of their parents' property. Sons and daughters alike received a marriage settlement and were able to establish independent households, no matter how poor, at a relatively early age.[11]

Motherhood stood as the cornerstone of a wife's importance within the family. In an agrarian society, children were economic assets, and a woman's fertility was vital to her family's survival. As the population grew in the pre-Famine period, therefore, a woman's importance as a mother and caretaker of children also increased. By 1841 the 1,934,298 women in Ireland between the ages of fifteen and forty-four were surrounded by 1,183,826 children under the age of four.[12]

A woman's importance within the family was also enhanced by her position as the provider of meals, a task that became increasingly difficult as poverty and dependence on the potato became more widespread. By 1830 the once diversified diet of cereals, fish, and dairy products had disappeared from most

Irish homes. As long as potatoes were plentiful, however, relatively high nutritional levels were maintained, as we have seen. Nevertheless, during the "hungry months" of the summer before the new harvest, and as potato blights recurred more regularly in the immediate pre-Famine period, entire meals consisted of meadow greens or seaweed gathered by the wife.[13]

The ability of women to earn wages added to their relatively high status before the Famine. Although the home was considered the proper sphere for a married woman, rigid distinctions between domestic duties and other types of work did not yet exist. Even as late as 1841, women composed over one half of the total agricultural labor force.[14] Poverty forced wives into far more diverse economic roles than those of mother or housekeeper only. Women's work was complementary to that of men, and women participated as coproducers within the family economy.

Women worked alongside men in fields, gathered seaweed for fertilizer (and sometimes for food), and carried peat for fuel home on their backs. They also tended the family's livestock, raised dairy animals and poultry and sold the products, distilled and marketed illicit whiskey, ran shops and inns, migrated at harvest time to work in England and Scotland, or oversaw farms while their husbands were working abroad. During the lean summer months, they took to the roads as beggars. In 1841 laborers' wives in Kerry could earn an average of a pound a year raising and selling a pig, and in nearby Limerick, noted an observer, "the wives keep fowls, and a woman can earn by the sale of eggs and fowls about 11s per annum." In that same year, a Royal Commission determined that between 18 and 31 percent of a family's income in Munster came from the sale of eggs, poultry, and the pig, each the economic responsibility of the wife. All told, even farms of fewer than five acres possessed an average of slightly less than one cow, slightly more than one sheep and one pig, and over seven hens apiece.[15] Since rents were paid in cash, women's wages from the sale of these farm animals and their products, as well as from a wide variety of other economic activities, were crucial sources of income for rural families.

Women's economic activities were so important that popular songs celebrated women's relationships with their cash-producing charges. One song tells the story of the "monster that murdered Nell Flaherty's drake." After describing the hapless bird (a legacy from her grandmother) as a "dear little fellow," with "legs [that] were yellow, . . . plump, fat, and heavy," Nell declares that she would "die for his sake." Lamenting its loss, Nell calls on the departed drake's "dozens of nephews and cousins" to avenge its untimely death. Furthermore, she places a curse on the murderer, hoping that "his turkeys never hatch, his pig never grunt" and "his cat never hunt." Although the song is humorous, there is no doubt about the seriousness of its intent. Nell and thousands of women like her ferociously defended their fowl, knowing that the income from these birds was critical to their families' survival.[16]

Perhaps the greatest single indicator of the importance of female economic activity was the simultaneous dwindling of cottage industry and the beginning of widespread poverty by 1830. In the subsistence economy, a woman's earnings from spinning, knitting, sewing, and lace making were crucial to a family's ability to stay on the land. According to one contemporary, "the men feed the family with their labor in the field, and the women pay the rent by spinning."[17]

This balance was permanently upset, however, when the mechanization of the textile industry and its rapid confinement to a narrow area of the northeast during the 1820s caused cheaper manufactured goods to flood the market and opportunities for paid labor from home production to disappear in most parts of Ireland. These changes in textile production were equal to the overpopulation factor in causing increasing poverty before the Famine, and they had especially severe consequences in the west, the region with the highest rates of population growth and the heaviest dependence on the potato. Since the cash incomes of women had delayed widespread seasonal migration from this region, the decreasing demand for female handiwork led to a rise in the number of seasonal migrants leaving the west. Between 1841, the year of the first official census, and 1851, the number of females over age fifteen earning wages from some form of the textile industry fell from one-half to one-quarter of their total number in the population.[18] Without women's wages, rents could not be paid.

Despite growing poverty in the first half of the nineteenth century, life in rural Ireland remained high spirited and leisure oriented. Since social activities and subsistence, not the pursuit of profit, dominated the traditional world view, the Irish enjoyed a yearlong series of celebrations and festivals. During the summer, communities joined together to bid farewell to emigrants. In the fall, harvest galas interrupted the routine of peasant life. In the winter, marriages took place. Throughout the year, fairs provided a festive atmosphere, as the Irish flocked to them to buy and sell animals, shop, court each other, or take part in factional fights—the almost ritualistic battles between competing families. At all times, drinking (and ether sniffing) enlivened social interactions. In fact, despite the growing poverty in the pre-Famine period, whiskey consumption was higher before the Famine than after it.[19]

Women in universally tight, low-necked bodices and red flannel skirts extending only halfway down their shins (for freedom of movement) mingled unchaperoned in the holiday crowds. They also took part in faction fights, often putting rocks in their stockings for use as weapons. They provided food and drink for the assembled celebrants—themselves included.[20]

Although some sexual segregation in social life did exist, male and female roles were far more fluid in the rough and tumble of life before the Famine than they would be later in the century. Conversation, sports, dancing, and seasonal celebrations, where women participated in the community's social and economic activities alongside men, brought variety to village life. Ironically, the very traditions that kept the Irish on the subsistence level helped foster social and economic partnerships between men and women.

In the space of the fifty years after 1830, however, traditional life disappeared everywhere in Ireland. Accelerated by the Famine, the demographic and economic changes that had begun in the north and the east in the 1830s spread throughout the country. By 1880 even peasants in the west were consolidating their land holdings and ending their reliance on a subsistence potato crop. These economic changes also meant the end of traditional social behavior. By the end of the post-Famine period, according to a woman in Donegal, "the sport and the recreation vanished. The poetry and the dancing came to an end. They forgot them and lost them, and when the good times came again, those things never came back as they were before."[21]

Although the material conditions of rural life changed after the Famine, land remained the center of the peasant economy. As subsistence farming and land fragmentation gave way to land consolidation and cash agriculture, livestock replaced potatoes as the primary agricultural product. By 1880 the farmer/landowner had replaced the tenant/landholder as the center of community life. By that year, the monetarization of the rural economy was complete.

The changing demographic and economic structure of rural Ireland had profound consequences for peasant cultural attitudes and, ultimately, for the position of women. Few outside of the the most prosperous classes delayed marriage early in the century on the expectation of improving their standard of living, but attitudes about the nature of marriage changed dramatically after the Famine, especially among those who had the greatest chance for economic improvement. As land consolidation and livestock raising created cash incomes and even profit for more and more farmers, marriage ceased to be based on romantic free attachment. Instead, it became an economic contract between the families of the bride and the groom to assure the continuity of descent and land ownership.[22]

As new economic patterns emerged, the arranged marriage became the accepted means of pairing a man and a woman. Brides had little prior knowledge of their husbands before their wedding day, and "there would be murder in the house if a girl were known to be friendly with a boy" before her marriage.[23] The glow of romance no longer eased a new wife's transition into her husband's home.

As a result, a dowry, not romance, determined a woman's ability to marry, and the desirability of the potential groom's farm was the greatest single determinant of dowry size. The fathers of the bride and groom negotiated the marriage contract, and neither the prospective spouses nor their mothers were consulted.[24] A woman's dowry was, therefore, controlled by her father and her father-in-law. She owned nothing in her own

right and remained economically dependent on the goodwill of
her male relatives.

The circular distribution of the woman's dowry helped rein-
force the increasingly patriarchal structure of the family. The
father was responsible for the dowering of only one of his daughters, not necessarily the oldest. The dowry originated with the
wife's father, and it was passed from father to father-in-law. If a
father died before dowering his daughter, his heir assumed the
responsibility for dowering his sister. The bride's dowry was
then used by her husband's family to dower the bride's sister-in-
law.[25] Nevertheless, because the early marriage of an heir
would prematurely displace his parents, many a son was reluctant "to bring another woman in on my mother."[26] Thus, many
sisters waited long years before receiving a sister-in-law's dowry
and thereby becoming eligible for their own marriage. Throughout their lives, women had no direct say in the complex recycling
of their inheritances.

As the nature of marriage changed, so did the structure of
family relationships. Before the Famine, husbands and wives
had shared a rough equality within the household. As arranged
marriages replaced romantic pairings, however, husbands felt
freer to exercise more authoritarian control over the family than
they had in the more democratic traditional family. And as
labor-intensive tillage disappeared, wives lost their importance
as agricultural producers, and their family position deteriorated. Furthermore, as domestic industry and other sources of
cash incomes for women disappeared, wives were no longer able
to generate valuable family income; they lost considerable status as a result.

Patriarchal authority within the family was also strengthened as the age gap between husbands and wives widened. In
the early nineteenth century, only 20 percent of husbands were
ten or more years older than their wives. By the early twentieth
century, fully 50 percent of husbands were at least ten years
older than their wives.[27] As the age gap between spouses grew,
so did the husband's power within the family. Not only had he
become the family's sole wage earner and controller of its economic assets and marital prospects, he now had much greater
maturity (and, supposedly, greater wisdom) than did his much

younger wife. By the third quarter of the nineteenth century, then, the husband had assumed full control over the lives of other family members in his roles as spouse, father, and owner of the family farm. As the head of the household, he alone determined how the the family's economic assets could be spent.

The relaxed interaction between men and women in traditional society also disappeared in the face of the new attitudes that arose out of demographic and economic change in the half century after 1830. As the arranged match replaced romance as the preferred prelude to matrimony, sex and procreation were subordinated to the family's economic well-being. Strict gender segregation and sexual puritanism both within the home and in the community as a whole replaced the friendly interaction formerly enjoyed by men and women in daily life. Beginning in infancy, and continuing even after marriage, males and females occupied separate spheres in their work and social activities. By the time of their marriages, men and women had had only a minimum of contact with members of the opposite sex.[28]

Since sexual behavior was governed by family considerations, a female's sexual misconduct was an economic matter. Accordingly, traditional sexual prohibitions became more exaggerated. Now, a young woman's fall from virtue not only ruined her family's name in the eyes of the community, but also threatened the family's economic well-being. In addition to causing her family's loss, the woman herself lost her social potential as a wife, now virtually her only avenue to economic security. Males were equally bound by community norms against premarital sex. Most Irish agreed that the sexual "misuse" of a girl was as bad as a landlord's economic exploitation, and a man who ruined a woman's reputation was universally censured.[29] "The no-good ones went out only with the no-good girls," remembered a male villager after his emigration.[30]

Premarital sex and illegitimacy were viewed in the same light, and romantic or recreational sex were horrors beyond the average peasant's ken. There was no toleration for sexual deviation, and young women who strayed from the prescribed path found no social safety nets for themselves or their illegitimate children. These sexual prohibitions were so well internalized that the already low pre-Famine illegitimacy rate fell even lower in the post-Famine period: although as many as 6 percent of all births recorded in 1835 had been out of wedlock, only 2 percent of all births between 1871 and 1880 were illegitimate.[31]

The Irish grew more devout after the trauma of the Famine, and the Catholic church grew more influential in shaping social attitudes as a result. Populated by priests and nuns from peasant families, the church lent its spiritual authority to the changing relationships between men and women. By preaching the virtues of celibacy and the reproductive purpose of the marriage bed, the church became an instrument of social control for the growing number of unmarried people in Ireland.[32] As one later emigrant recalled, "It was a mortal sin if you didn't do what the priest said. You were damned to hell."[33]

The church also reinforced the subordination of women in the new society emerging after 1850. Priests emphasized the idea that women were the occasions of sin and that they were "deadly perils [causing] the difficulty of temporal life."[34] The church also promoted the idea that a woman's place was in the home. In 1881 a leading churchman proclaimed that no one should "tolerate . . . the woman who . . . disavows her birthright of modesty to parade herself before the public gaze."[35] The patriarchal church, therefore, now reflected the needs of the increasingly patriarchal peasant family. Motherhood remained the sole acceptable expression of a woman's sexuality, and unmarried women were to choose celibacy as an article of religion. Since over 90 percent of the Catholic population regularly attended Mass by the early 1880s,[36] the church's teachings were influential indeed in promoting women's newly fashioned subordination.

Women were affected more than men by the intensified sexual segregation of post-Famine society. Although unmarried men also experienced long, and often permanent, periods of celibacy, they, unlike women, were permitted a public life. For instance, as subsistence agriculture disappeared, unemployed men replaced women in such traditionally female jobs as dairying and poultry raising. Between 1841 and 1911, the number of farm workers fell from over one-half to less than one-third of the employed population. By 1911 only one in twelve of this much reduced work force was female.[37] Moreover, while social networks outside of the home existed for men, none developed for women. Women's lives had become so narrow, in fact, that their attendance at mass on Sundays was their only opportunity to mingle with neighbors. According to one villager, "After their day's work ended, the men played skittles or billiards at the club . . . [but] the women had no club."[38]

The declining position of women in rural Ireland in the half-century before 1880 can also be measured in terms of female mortality. While longevity for all the Irish increased as economic conditions improved, the excess female longevity over that of males decreased. As a result, while life expectancies for both men and women almost doubled between 1841 and 1880—rising from 26.0 to 49.4 years for males and 27.0 to 49.9 years for females—the excess of female over male life expectancy fell from twelve months to only five months in those same years. In addition, as female economic productivity fell, girls received less and less of the family's food supply. Throughout the lean years of the 1860s and 1870s, more girls than boys under age nineteen died each year.[39]

These developments brought about changes in women's attitudes. "I had two choices . . . to marry or go into service again. I was sick and tired of . . . service and I thought it would be better for me to have a man . . . and someone to protect me, and to own a house too, where I could sit down at my ease," wrote a woman of her young adulthood in Dingle in the late nineteenth century.[40] Although this woman did find a husband, by 1880, when all of Ireland had been transformed from a subsistence into a cash economy, fully two-thirds of all the women over age fifteen in the country were unmarried and unable to find a man to "protect" them from the harsh reality of their diminished social and economic status. The combination of economic reorganization and expanding contact with the outside world, however, created new attitudes in conflict with peasant values. After the Famine, these attitudes had become widespread enough that women grew less and less content with the discrepancy between their rising expectations and their dependent positions on family farms.

The national schools were one of the most important vehicles for bringing cultural change to rural Ireland. This system of public primary education—the first in the British Isles—was created by Parliament in 1831.[41] Since the government wished to use the schools as a means to end traditional culture in Ireland, educational materials emphasized British middle-class values. School readers presented "Paddy" and "Bridey" as intellectually incompetent, violent, drunken, and slovenly, drifting into poverty because of early marriage and indiscriminate reproduction. Teachers emphasized order and cleanliness at the expense of reading, writing, and arithmetic, although vocational training—agricultural theory for boys and needlework for girls—was also offered.[42]

But despite the government's active attempt to alter the patterns of traditional life, the national schools had little impact on peasant attitudes before the Famine. Since employers of agricultural laborers opposed state-supported schools, primary education was not made compulsory until the late nineteenth century. Furthermore, although peasants generally favored sending their children to the national schools, secondary schools remained private (and therefore too expensive for the average parent) until the late 1870s. There was almost no higher education for Catholics until the twentieth century.[43]

So, although illiteracy fell after 1831 with the introduction of the national schools, the majority of the Irish still could not read or write on the eve of the Famine. In 1840 only 1,973 schools existed in all of Ireland, and only 232,560 children—a tiny fraction of the school-age population—were enrolled in them. Further, only 100,000 children attended school on a daily basis in that year. By 1841, after a full decade of state-sponsored education, more than one-half of the total population over age five remained illiterate. Since Catholic speakers of Irish had the highest illiteracy rates of all, in 1841 fully 72 percent of the population of Connaught—the province with the highest proportion of this group in its population—could neither read nor write.[44]

The persistence of the use of the Irish rather than the English language among large segments of the peasant population is another indication of the limited influence of the national schools before the Famine. Although school lessons were taught in English and the peasants were not opposed to learning that language, Irish remained the mother tongue for many. In fact, in 1840, partly because of rapid population growth, more spoke Irish than ever before or since. By 1851 one-quarter of the population still spoke Irish, especially in the most densely populated regions of the west and the southwest. In that year, while only 3.5 and 6.8 percent of the populations of Leinster and Ulster spoke Irish, fully 43.9 and 50.8 percent of the populations of Munster and Connaught continued to do so.[45]

Eventually, however, the national schools did become an important factor in ending the isolation of the traditional peasant. Primary education to age twelve became compulsory in 1876, and the Intermediate Education Act of 1878 established a system of secondary schools throughout the country. Although secondary education remained costly, and therefore out of the reach of most Irish, interest in education was abetted by the new laws. Between 1870 and 1900, the number of local primary schools increased from 6,806 to 8,684. In these same years, the average daily attendance in the growing number of schools rose from 359,119 to 770,622 children, despite rapid population decrease.[46]

As a result of the growing influence of primary education in the last half of the nineteenth century, the number of Irish over the age of five who could neither read nor write fell by one-third, from 47 percent to 14 percent of their total number in the population.[47] Perhaps even more significantly, as the demand for female labor decreased, girls were able to devote more of their childhoods to school. Accordingly, female illiteracy rates fell even more quickly than did those of males in the late nineteenth century. For example, in 1871, 37.5 percent of all grooms and 45.2 percent of all brides signed their marriage certificates with an X, an indication of their inability to read or write even their own names. By 1901, however, while 13.2 percent of all grooms still signed the marriage register with an X, only 10.7 percent of the brides did so. These figures tell us that illiteracy decreased among brides by over one-third in the three decades after 1871, while it decreased among grooms by only one-quarter in the same thirty years. Even more telling is the fact that although many more females than males were illiterate upon marriage in 1871, the opposite was true in 1901.[48]

Girls also attended school in greater number and with greater enthusiasm than did boys. In 1900 there were 2,244 female schools and only 1,973 male schools, and attendance among girls in the additional 4,467 coeducational schools in Ireland in that year was higher than that among boys.[49] Males also recalled their school days with far less fondness than females. "I was going to school every day . . . the seven tasks of the mountain on me as I thought," one man remembered. "Before long it seemed to me there was nobody in the world had a worse life than myself."[50] Another wrote, "the school was . . . a harsh . . . place to be in."[51] In contrast, a woman recalled her first day of school in glowing terms. "Monday arrived," she explained, "and I was in great form because I was going to school . . . I like[d] it very much."[52]

Whether they enjoyed school or not, however, both men and women remembered the excellence of their Irish educations. One native of County Clare was taught "all subjects. We had . . . science, languages, math, . . . history."[53] One of his contemporaries, also from County Clare, was equally well educated. According to his daughter, "[He] had a wonderful education . . . [He] got a good background in reading, writing, and arithmetic . . . [and] poems—[He] could recite poems, all kinds."[54] Other children of Irish immigrants to the United States also recall their parents' pride in their education. One son remembered his Irish-born mother's habit of blessing herself before she signed her Social Security check: "She thanked God that she was able to write her own name on that check."[55] Unlike most of their contemporaries leaving other areas of agricultural Europe, Irish emigrants, especially the females, were equipped with the literacy demanded by their new urban environments.

The impact of national education in the late nineteenth century can also be seen in the decreasing number of Irish-speaking people. Although one-quarter of the Irish and one-half of the population of Connaught spoke the language in 1851, only 14.4 percent of the total population and 38.0 percent of the population of the west still did so by 1901.[56]

Contemporaries noted the change. Recalling the results of his first year in school, a man remembered that "there was hardly a word of Irish [left] in my mouth . . . only English."[57] Another student in the late nineteenth century later offered this observation: "Older people were always complaining that they were looked down on because they had [no] English. So I was sent to school." Remembering the humiliation of his first day of school, he added, "I hadn't a single word of English, no more than anyone else in my family, and I couldn't answer the master when he asked me . . . my name."[58] One young girl, afraid of not understanding the English of the teacher on the first day of school, was reassured by her friend. "I have English," her friend told her, "I'll tell you what the schoolmissus is saying."[59] But, as Mary Ann Donovan recalled, by the late nineteenth century, parents and teachers, even in the west, discouraged children from using Irish.[60]

By the turn of the twentieth century, government schools had been so successful in ending the use of the Irish language that Nationalists made the reintroduction of the Irish language a hallmark of their crusade to free Irish culture from English domination. These efforts were in vain for the most part, however. Although he "had to learn everything . . . in Gaelic and English," an Irish immigrant to the United States remembered, he soon forgot the Gaelic once he left school.[61]

Improved transportation and communication networks also helped acquaint the rural population with new ideas from the outside world after the Famine. Although roads and canals had existed since the eighteenth century, and the first railroad in Ireland extended the few miles from Dublin to Kingstown by 1834, most of rural Ireland remained untouched by these transportation advances until the end of the pre-Famine period. Nevertheless, by the 1840s only the most remote coastal areas in the west were more than ten miles from some form of public transportation. By the 1860s all the regions of Ireland were connected by railroad.[62]

Contact with the outside world was also enhanced by the introduction of the penny post in 1840. In earlier years, the cost of sending a letter from Dublin to Cork had been equal to an agricultural laborer's daily wage.[63] Further, because so few could read or write in English before 1850, there had been little demand for newspapers and magazines. After the Famine, however, newspapers and other periodicals grew in number and popularity as transportation advances reduced their cost and English literacy increased. By 1879 even Connaught boasted eighteen newspapers.[64] Letters from emigrants abroad also contributed to the expanding cultural horizons of the rural Irish after the Famine. As one widely read periodical editorialized, "the Irish girl who has gone to America sends home photographs of herself. It is these photographs that do all the mischief with her remaining sisters. . . . Is this fashionably attired lady the Bridget they knew?"[65] Or, as an immigrant in the United States wrote to his aunt in Carlow, "This is a good place for smart young boys and girls [who] wish to go in situations. . . . Any boy or girl who has to labour for their living, this is the country for them. . . . Girls can get 8 to 14 pounds per year."[66]

In addition to cash incomes and ready employment, rural youth was also enticed by the promise of marriage in America. As one Irishman in Minnesota wrote to his cousin in Ireland, "women of all kinds are rather scarce here. . . . Pick out one for me and [I] will pay her passage. I . . . have two good horses, four cows, eight sheep, twenty hogs and all the tools to work my farm. I am a carpenter to boot and will give her all the tea and coffee and pork she can possibly [want]."[67] Though business in mail-order brides was never very brisk, letters like these brought enticing news of the outside world to women in rural Ireland in the last half of the nineteenth century. Reading such letters, unmarried, unemployed girls grew ever more dissatisfied with their status at home.

The economic recovery and the introduction of materialistic and individualistic values in the fifty years preceding 1880 fostered a steady decline in the status of Irish women; they created an awareness that the circumstances of women's lives did not match the promise of their aspirations. By 1885 this conflict between a new reality and rising expectations caused more and more women to seek a new direction in their lives by emigrating.

CHAPTER THREE

Women and Emigration 1880-1920

As women's awareness of the gap between the realities of their lives and the opportunities available to them in the outside world grew in the course of the nineteenth century, more and more chose emigration over celibate dependency on family farms. By 1885, and continuing into the twentieth century, unmarried women dominated emigration out of Ireland. As one woman who emigrated in the 1880s explained,"[I] used to live on a farm . . . in Ireland and it was hard work there. . . . There were five in our family and they all worked on the farm. . . . My sister and myself . . . just packed up one day and came to America."[1]

The mass exodus of surplus women was the culmination of nineteenth-century Irish emigration. Throughout the period, emigration patterns reflected the changes in Irish life in terms of the place of origin, economic class, sex, and marital status of the emigrant majority. For the growing number of landless and unmarried young people after 1830, emigration provided relief from worsening conditions at home and a route to an independent adult status abroad. Unmarried women from the west and the southwest were the last in this succession of the newly dispossessed to emigrate in large numbers.

By 1830, as economic conditions deteriorated everywhere in Ireland, pessimism about the country's future deepened, and for good reason. In thirteen out of the seventeen years between 1828 and 1845 the potato crop failed somewhere in the country. In 1832 cholera afflicted the peasantry everywhere on the island. And throughout the period, endemic agrarian violence threatened life and limb. As famine, disease, and unrest stalked the countryside, a sense of doom penetrated the collective consciousness. As one farmer wrote, "the mizerable world seems to

be tottering to its centre." Another agreed, predicting that
"there is a Distruction Aproaching . . . Ireland . . . thire time is
nerely at an end."[2]

In addition to apocalyptic prophesies, other indicators at-
tested to the dire straits of the pre-Famine economy. By the
1820s the contraction of the domestic textile industry brought
on by the introduction of mechanization left thousands of cottage workers suddenly without work. By 1826 more than ten
thousand weavers were unemployed in Belfast alone. Elsewhere, the domestic textile industry disappeared entirely,[3] leaving thousands of peasant producers without the cash income
needed to pay the rent on their holdings. According to one
former weaver in 1829, "We are . . . actually famishing from
want of employment. . . . we are . . . deprived of any hope of
existence, and see no prospect but in emigration."[4]

Nevertheless, poverty did not lead to permanent emigration
before the Famine. In the first half of the nineteenth century,
the average annual income of an agricultural laborer (the growing majority of the male population) was between £10 and £15,
and passage to the United States, the most popular emigrant
destination, cost as much as £12.[5] Most of the Irish in those years
were too poor to leave the country permanently.

The highest emigration rates before the Famine, therefore,
appeared in the relatively prosperous north and east, the areas
where a cash economy still existed and the trend toward population control had already begun. As A.C. Buchanan, the British
government's emigration agent in Quebec, reported in the late
1820s, "the bulk of emigrants [are] first, the small farmer [who]
disposes of his interest [in his holding], by which he raises a
little money. . . . The second . . . , artisans."[6] Conversely, the
lowest emigration rates were in the south and west, the poorest
regions in the country. These were also the areas with the
highest population increases and the greatest reliance on subsistence potato cultivation.

Before 1845 population movement in Munster and Connaught remained mostly temporary. As sources of supplementary income at home disappeared, the poorer rural population
was forced to travel abroad during the summer months to earn
cash wages with which to pay the rent on their holdings. As a

result, seasonal migration figures reveal a geographical distribution different from that shown by permanent emigration
figures. According to the Census of 1841, 25,118 of the 57,651
seasonal migrants in that year came from Connaught, fully
10,430 from the county of Mayo alone.[7] The low rate of permanent emigration from the west between 1780 and 1845 and the
high rate of seasonal migration after 1830 indicate the increased
reliance of the population there on subsistence potato cultivation.

During the first half of the Famine decade of 1845 to 1855,
relative prosperity remained a precondition to permanent emigration, and regional differences in emigration patterns persisted as a result. Between 1845 and 1851, therefore, farmers and
urban craftsmen, along with their families, from Ulster and
Leinster continued as the emigrant majority.[8] Contemporaries
noted the loss of the "better class of our population," and la-
mented that "the obvious strength of our country is departing."[9]

After 1851, however, emigraton took on the appearance of
wholesale flight from "fever, and disease and hunger, with
money scarcely sufficient to pay passage for the voyage."[10]
Believing "they could not be worse off in America," more and
more Irish insisted that "all we want is to get out of Ireland."[11]
As the number of ships crossing the Atlantic and the Irish Sea
increased in the early 1850s, the peak years of nineteenth-
century emigration, and as accommodations on these "coffin
ships" deteriorated, the cost of passage also fell. Now the landless could afford the £3 passage to America, or the almost
destitute the few pence needed to set sail for Britain. These
lowered costs, coupled with the simultaneous spread of land
consolidation into Munster, meant that displaced agricultural
laborers and their families in that province, the single largest
emigrant group between 1851 and 1855, could now achieve the
"joyful deliverance" of passage abroad.[12] Sadly, although the
heaviest Famine mortality occurred in Connaught, it remained
the province with the least emigration.

Informed that a man "can save more [money in the United
States while] learning his trade than [in Ireland] after his time
being served,"[13] displaced laborers in the south, north, and east
continued as the emigrant majority after the Famine. In all the

years between 1855 and 1880, however, emigration from the west stayed the lowest in Ireland. There, seasonal, rather than permanent, migration indicated the persistence of traditional demographic and economic practices. As a result, the number of seasonal migrants from that region almost doubled between 1841 and the mid-1860s, rising from 60,000 to 100,000 annually.[14]

In all, emigration before 1880 was heaviest in areas where market agriculture had replaced labor-intensive tillage, thereby reducing the number of people needed to make the land productive. Permanent emigration continued to have the same negative correlation with subsistence farming after the Famine that it had had before and during it.

Only in the late 1870s, as famine once again appeared in western areas still dependent on the potato, and as demand for seasonal labor decreased under the impact of mechanized farming, did population control and land consolidation become accepted in the west and the southwest. By 1880 permanent emigration from these regions began to increase, despite population decline. Consequently, while Ireland as a whole saw lower emigration after 1890, mostly because of overall population loss, emigration rates from Connaught continued to increase into the twentieth century. Although Munster, followed by Ulster, had the largest numbers of emigrants between 1881 and 1920, by 1911 Connaught had the highest emigration rate in the country, as it too transformed its traditional way of life.[15]

As emigration from the west and the southwest rose after 1880, population decline in these regions became ever more noticeable. Between 1881 and 1926, while Leinster and Ulster lost one-tenth of their populations, and Munster one-quarter, Connaught's population fell by one-third.[16] As one man explained, emigration "didn't break up the family, but it geographically dispersed the family. . . . There was nothing else to do really. . . . Couples that got married had families of eight, ten, twelve, . . . sixteen . . . you can imagine what it would have been like if all those people had stayed. . . . The country wouldn't be able to support them. So you'd have a continuous famine."[17]

By the late 1850s a new variable in the decision to emigrate—

Table 3: Excess Female Emigration by Province, Ireland,
1851-1855

Province	Total Emigration	Excess Females
Leinster	171,201	− 817
Munster	296,531	+ 8,429
Ulster	175,151	− 4,829
Conaught	97,709	+ 1,137
Ireland	740,592	+ 3,970

Source: Censuses for Ireland, 1851-1855, in *Irish Historical Statistics,* table
58, pp. 344-53.

that of sex—became increasingly marked. As more and more
young women lost the opportunity to marry and thereby assume
an adult social and economic role, the emigration of daughters
and sisters of farmers and laborers rose.

Nevertheless, before 1885 most of those leaving Ireland had
been male. Although the sex ratio among permanent emigrants
before the Famine had been fairly evenly balanced, seasonal
migrants, who were almost always male, vastly outnumbered
permanent emigrants in the first half of the nineteenth century,
especially from the west and the south.[18] Furthrmore, males
regained the majority among emigrants during the Famine
decade of 1845 to 1855.

But after 1850, more women than men left certain provinces
in certain years, as can be seen in table 3. Between 1851 and
1855, females outnumbered males among emigrants from
Munster and Connaught, and in the years 1853 and 1855, an
overall female emigrant majority existed. This excess female
emigration was not necessarily a migration of single women,
however. Rather, it often represented a traditional female emigration pattern of a woman's following a male relative's earlier
journey abroad. As a Dublin shipper reported, "the general
custom is, that when a family is about to emigrate, two or three
of the youngest and strongest go first, and then, when they
obtain footing, they send for the rest of the family."[19] Although
daughters could be among the "two or three youngest and
strongest" in the family, the entire family, parents included,

Table 4: Excess Male Emigration by Province, Ireland,
1855-1884

Province	Total Emigration	Excess Males
Leinster	390,994	+ 23,400
Munster	739,878	+ 45,050
Ulster	716,770	+105,534
Connaught	312,557	− 341
Ireland	2,160,199	+173,643

Source: Censuses for Ireland, 1855-1884, in *Irish Historical Statistics,* Table
58, pp. 344-53.

eventually joined them abroad. Accordingly, even if young women temporarily escaped the bonds of familial authority
through emigration, they were soon joined by their families in
their new homes. No permanent break from parental supervi-
sion occurred.

In the late 1850s, the emigration of single women grew even
more common as their proportion in the population increased
with the spread of land consolidation and new inheritance patterns. Nevertheless, despite the emigration of more and more
unmarried women after the Famine, men regained the lead in
overall emigration totals after 1855, as can be seen in table 4.
Significant regional variations in emigrant sex ratios did exist,
however. For instance, between 1855 and 1884, males consis-
tently outnumbered females among those leaving Leinster,
Munster, and Ulster. In Connaught, on the other hand, females
outnumbered males among permanent emigrants in twenty out
of the twenty-nine years between 1855 and 1884.[20] This excess
female emigration from the west after the Famine is deceptive,
nonetheless. At all times until the 1870s, male seasonal migrants continued to outnumber by far permanent emigrants
among those departing from the west.

In addition, the proportion of males among emigrants rose
with each decade in the post-Famine period. Throughout the
late 1850s, over 50 percent of all emigrants were male, rising to
54 percent in 1858. As bad weather ruined crops in the early
1860s, many of the poorest men in the west left to fight in the

American Civil War. These men, according to the U.S. consul at Galway, "wo[uld] gladly embrace any opportunity of removal from the misery and starvation they are enduring here." By the 1870s and early 1880s, 55 percent of those leaving Ireland were the consul's "strong young men . . . who sigh for food and employment in the US."[21]

As we know, females regained the lead in emigration totals in the mid-1880s. Between 1885 and 1920, females outnumbered males among the 1.4 million people leaving Ireland by almost twenty thousand. This female emigrant majority was a reflection of the economic downswing in the United States in those years.[22] While male emigration rates were tied to the fluctuating prosperity of U. S. industry, those of women were not, for they could readily find work as domestic servants in U. S. cities. As a result, although men continued to leave Ireland in the late nineteenth and early twentieth centuries, more and more women followed in Julia Lough's footsteps. Writing from Winsted, Connecticut, to her sister in Ireland, Julia exulted, "I am very glad I made the change. . . . [Emigrating] was what I always wanted. . . . I have reached my highest ambition."[23]

Irish emigrants had always tended to be young, and after 1885 they became ever younger. More than half of all those who left Ireland between 1880 and 1916 were aged fifteen to twenty-five. The female emigrant majority in the late nineteenth and early twentieth centuries was even more pronounced among the youngest emigrants, as girls left home earlier and in greater number than boys. Females greatly outnumbered males among emigrants aged fifteen to nineteen (the youngest emigrant age group on emigration returns) between 1885 and 1920, as they had in every year since 1855. Females also slightly outnumbered males in the largest single emigrant age group, that of twenty to twenty-five, after 1885. Altogether, almost 82,000 more females than males aged fifteen to twenty-five left Ireland between 1885 and 1920.[24]

This excess female emigration stemmed from several long-term changes in Irish demographic and economic life, as we have seen. By the early 1880s these changes had penetrated even the most remote areas of the west and the southwest. There, the emigration of women rose as they abruptly lost their

Table 5: Excess Female Emigration by Province, Ireland,
1885-1920

Province	Total Female Emigration	Excess Females
Leinster	87,298	– 13,514
Munster	241,118	+ 7,465
Ulster	174,735	– 20,333
Connaught	182,502	+ 44,628
Ireland	685,653	+ 18,296

Source: Censuses for Ireland, 1885-1920, in *Irish Historical Statistics*, table 58, pp. 345-53.

potential to become wives and producers within the family economy. As can be seen in table 5, except for the anomalous war decade after 1911, when most female emigrants came from Ulster, female emigration between 1885 and 1920 was highest from Munster and Connaught, and lowest from Leinster and Ulster, the regions that had adjusted to the exigencies of economic reorganization much earlier in the nineteenth century.

With little to keep them at home, young girls left their homeland by the thousands. According to one young woman who emigrated at the time, "There was nothing to be gained by remaining at home. . . . So I realized that [it] would be better for me to turn a penny for myself and not to depend on anyone else."[25] Furthermore, as young women lost their demographic and economic importance in peasant society, they were more likely than boys to be "trained" to emigrate by staying in school longer and thereby acquiring the literacy needed to succeed in urban environments abroad.

Perhaps the most telling indication of the impact of demographic and economic change on emigration patterns was the steadily increasing number of unmarried women among those leaving the country from the 1850s forward. By the late nineteenth and early twentieth centuries, as restricted marriage and market agriculture penetrated even the remotest areas of the west, almost 90 percent of all female emigrants aged fifteen to thirty-five were single, as can be seen in table 6.

Table 6: Percentage of Unmarried Female Emigrants Aged
Fifteen to Thirty-Five, Ireland, 1885-1920[a]

Years	Leinster	Munster	Ulster	Connaught	Total
1885-1890	83.2	85.5	88.3	93.8	87.7
1891-1900	89.4	93.7	88.6	96.5	92.1
1901-1908	90.9	95.6	77.2	97.9	90.4
1912, 1918, 1920	81.0	91.9	73.9	91.9	84.7
Total	86.1	91.7	82.0	95.0	88.7

Source: Emigration Statistics of Ireland, 1885-1920.
[a]1909-11,1913-17,1919 figures not available.

Although the migration of unmarried women after 1885 was
not a new phenomenon in Irish emigration history, before the
Famine most women emigrated within families as wives or
daughters. Unmarried women, if they left home at all, tended to
migrate to towns within Ireland rather than travel abroad. In
fact, by 1841 women significantly outnumbered men in Irish
towns and cities. But urban employment opportunities for women did not expand, and as one observer noticed, the ranks of
prostitutes were increasing as many an otherwise unemployed
woman, "through necessity, perambulate[s] the streets."[26] As
we shall see, Irish cities ceased to attract rural migrants by
midcentury because of such conditions.

Families continued to dominate emigration during the Famine. Husbands and wives either left together, or husbands emigrated alone, later sending for their wives. By the early 1850s, as
we have seen, the emigration of wives joining their husbands
already abroad raised overall female emigration totals consider-
ably.[27]

Beginning in the mid-1850s and continuing into the early
1880s, as the worst ravages of the Famine abated and as the
patterns of delayed and restricted marriage spread, fewer nuclear families emigrated, and single adults became more numerous among the people leaving Ireland. Though unmarried
males in their early twenties constituted the majority of these

emigrants, young single women became more numerous over time.

A major demographic shift occurred after 1880 when the marriage patterns prevailing in the north and the east modified and the patterns of delayed and restricted marriage in the west and the southwest intensified. As a result, while the overall rate for marriage rose from a low of 3.6 per 1,000 in the population to 6.0 per 1,000 in the population between 1880 and 1920, it fell in the west and the southwest in those same years. By 1900 the oldest marriage ages and the lowest marriage rates were found in Connaught and western Munster.[28] Altogether, two-thirds of the Irish in the four decades after 1880 never married.[29]

The overall percentage of unmarried people between the ages of fifteen and forty-four, the prime years for marrying and for emigrating, was even higher in the late nineteenth and early twentieth centuries than it was among the population as a whole. An average of 70 percent of this age group was single between 1880 and 1920.[30] Furthermore, the proportion of the population within this age group actually rose between 1881 and 1901. By 1926 fully 41 percent of the population was between these ages.[31]

The increases within the total population in the percentages of Irish of marriageable age after 1881 were especially high in the west and the southwest, the regions that had more or less abruptly adopted the new demographic and economic patterns of delayed and restricted marriage and land consolidation in the late 1870s. In contrast, their percentage in the total population fell after 1881 in many areas of the north and the east.[32] In addition, while the overall percentage of women within this age group declined after 1901 (reflecting their high rates of emigration), that of males remained stable until 1911.

As the proportion of the unmarried in the overall population remained high in the late nineteenth and early twentieth centuries, unwed women became the largest single emigrant category for the first time. Between 1885 and the First World War, the number of these women emigrating from all provinces except Ulster increased in all years, and single women outnumbered married women in all age groups between fifteen and thirty. In addition, the total number of married women overall, especially among female emigrants aged thirty to thirty-five, decreased. This unmarried female emigrant majority was especially pronounced among those leaving Munster and Connaught.[33] During the First World War, a slight shift occurred, as married women became a larger percentage of the much reduced number of females leaving Ireland. This was a temporary change, however, reflecting the abnormalities of wartime rather than a new trend. By the end of the war, single women once again outnumbered married women among females leaving the country.[34]

Women's emigration in the late nineteenth and early twentieth centuries represented a transitional stage in their social and economic modernization, a process that had been curtailed by the demographic and economic retrenchments after 1830. The anomalous patterns found in Irish emigration between 1885 and 1920 were the result of the incomplete modernization of Irish society in those years. Changing rural communities could accommodate some, but not all, of the rising expectations brought about by mass literacy and improvements in the standard of living, transportation, and communication while still remaining intact. Consequently, women who wished to marry or to earn independent incomes were compelled to leave their birthplaces and emigrate abroad. Their home communities held no promise of a better future. As one emigrant concluded, "there were five in the family and the farm was only enough to support one."[35]

As a result, two-thirds of a million young, usually unmarried women left Ireland in the late nineteenth and early twentieth centuries, seeking opportunities unavailable to them at home. Since daughters were even less able to find alternative means of support at home than were sons, they emigrated in even greater numbers than their brothers. As one son of an Irish-born woman who had emigrated in the 1890s remembered, "[My grandfather] died. The older children were all girls [who] couldn't work the farm . . . and there were no boys to work it so that was it . . . they came [to America]."[36]

These young women who left Ireland in the late nineteenth and early twentieth centuries departed with mixed emotions, however. Although many saw their journey as a step to a new and more exciting life, others were frightened at the prospect of leaving their homes and friends for a strange new environment abroad. Therefore, while one female emigrant acknowledged that "we had known Americans . . . and they always struck us as being sort of like ourselves . . . they looked the same as us, they behaved the same . . . as us,"[37] another recalled that "the first few years of my life [in the United States] I was rather homesick . . . [but] I knew I was better situated [there] than I would be in Roscommon."[38]

Clearly, these girls were pulled as much as pushed out of the Ireland of their youth. The woman who left Roscommon summed up the reason for the migration of her generation: "We were a very large family . . . we all worked on [our parents'] farm. . . . As we grew older, . . . the girls . . . became a little wiser and realized that our town did not afford much financially . . . [so] I came to America."[39]

CHAPTER FOUR

The Impact of Women's Emigration 1880-1920

The emigration of almost 700,000 women between 1885 and 1920, although the result of a half century of change, retarded further innovation at home. Rural society, freed from the potentially disruptive influence of a large number of surplus women, clung to patterns of life that were no longer socially or economically beneficial. In fact, the cash remittances sent home by sisters and daughters already abroad perpetuated in rural Ireland the obsolete patterns of life that had prompted mass female emigration in the first place. As a result, female emigration continued and continuing depopulation inhibited economic growth. As economic stagnation replaced economic recovery, women's diminished status at home remained unchanged, despite the mass exodus of their sisters.

The loss of so many young women from rural Ireland was a major factor in the persistent decrease in population in the countryside. In the four decades after 1881, the population fell by almost one fifth, going from 5.2 million to 4.2 million. By 1926, the first year of official census taking after independence, the population measured only one-half of its 1845 peak of 8.5 million. As more and more women left the country after 1885, the female majority in the population also began to erode. After 1911 females were the minority sex in Ireland for the first time since accurate records had been kept (see table 7).

The male surplus in the population was first noticeable in the west and southwest, the areas with the highest rate of female emigration after 1885. As early as 1891, Munster, the province with the largest number of female emigrants in the late nineteenth and early twentieth centuries, had more males than females in its population. By 1901 more males than females

Table 7: Excess Female Population, Ireland, 1881-1926

Year	Total Population	Excess Females
1881	5,174,836	+ 108,282
1891	4,704,750	+ 66,884
1901	4,458,775	+ 58,695
1911	4,390,219	+ 6,123
1926	4,228,553	− 1,401

Source: Censuses for Ireland, 1881-1926, in *Irish Historical Statistics,* table 3, p. 3.

lived in Connaught also, again reflecting the high rate of female emigration from that province after 1885. Conversely, females remained the majority sex in Ulster (except for the three counties that joined the Free State—the most rural in the province) and Leinster, the provinces with the lowest rate of female emigration in the late nineteenth and early twentieth centuries, as can be seen in table 8.

The parish register in Knockainy Parish in Limerick once again mirrored overall population trends. Between 1901 and 1926, female population losses in the parish were greater than those for males. While the male population fell by 9.2 percent, the female population fell by 14.7 percent. Although females had outnumbered males by 794 to 753 in 1901, by 1926, 684 males and only 678 females remained in Knockainy.[1]

Even before 1911 males outnumbered females in the younger age groups in the population, reflecting the higher female mortality rates among infants and children. Since daughters had less economic potential than sons, they were considered more expendable in times of scarcity, such as the near famine of the late 1870s. Consequently, girls were given less food, and they suffered other physical deprivations in these bleak seasons. As a result, between 1881 and 1920, an average death rate of 111.5 females for each 100 males aged five to nine existed. Among children between ten and fourteen, the death rate in those years averaged 133 females for each 100 males.[2] The higher female mortality among children meant that after 1880 boys outnumbered girls from birth to age fourteen everywhere in Ireland.

Table 8. Excess Female Population by Province, Ireland, 1881-1926

Year	Leinster	Munster	Ulster	Connaught
1881	+ 18,913	+ 11,127	+ 70,627	+ 7,815
1891	+ 12,066	− 2,820	+ 57,156	+ 442
1901	+ 9,211	− 5,752	+ 45,838	− 402
1911	+ 6,110	− 16,765	+ 39,972	− 13,194
1926	+ 1,292	− 17,354	− 9,725[a]	− 15,999

Source: Censuses for Ireland, 1881-1926, in *Irish Historical Statistics*, tables 6 and 7, pp. 15, 16, 24.
[a]Three Free State counties only.

The girls who did survive were far more likely to emigrate than boys.

The emigration of girls at younger ages than boys also affected the sex ratios among the younger population. As can be seen in table 9, in all the years after 1881 except 1901, females were the minority sex up to age twenty-four, even though they were the majority of the overall population until after 1911.

In addition, the figures in table 9 demonstrate that the excess female population over age twenty-five fell dramatically after 1881. This decrease cannot be totally explained by the overall population loss in the late nineteenth and early twentieth centuries. Rather, the continuation of abnormally high female infant and child mortality, as is indicated by the relative stability of male numerical superiority among this age group, coupled with the persistence of high emigration rates among young women in those years, meant that fewer and fewer adult women remained in Ireland into the twentieth century.

Continuing patterns of delayed and restricted marriage also contributed to population decline in the late nineteenth and early twentieth centuries. Although one-third of all women between 1881 and 1920 were aged fifteen to thirty-four, almost three-quarters of those within this age group were unmarried. Of these unmarried women, almost one in three emigrated in those years.[3] Since most female emigrants in the late nineteenth and early twentieth centuries were in their prime reproductive years, persistent population decline, despite the

Table 9: Excess Male Population by Age, Ireland, 1881-1911

| | Age | | |
Year	0-14	15-24	25+
1881	+29,466	-24,678	-1,113,070
1891	+26,257	+ 5,928	- 99,029
1901	+21,782	-12,397	- 68,180
1911	+20,815	+13,245	- 39,183

Source: Censuses for Ireland, 1881-1920, in *Irish Historical Statistics,* table 25, pp. 78-81.

maintenance of high marital fertility, was inevitable. Therefore, although the number of births fell only gradually after 1881, the population fell dramatically. As more and more women left the country, not only did overall population decrease, but the potential for population growth or even maintenance disappeared, as can be seen in table 10.

Although population decline had accelerated the transition from subsistence to market agriculture, post-Famine economic recovery had depended on a delicate balance between depopulation and land consolidation rather than on any far-reaching alterations in either agriculture or industry. As we have seen, falling population levels had helped prevent the expansion of Irish manufacture after the Famine. Furthermore, although depopulation had fostered agricultural recovery after 1850, renewed prosperity was not shared equally by all social classes in all regions of the country.

Since the patterns of land ownership remained unchanged throughout the third quarter of the nineteenth century, the consolidation of land holdings that had made possible the conversion to profitable pasturage also led to the dispossession of agricultural laborers. By the late 1870s a combination of bad harvests and new competition on the international market caused a decrease in both agricultural production and prices. Irish farmers were no longer competitive, as cheaper American grain and Dutch and Danish dairy products flooded British and domestic markets.[4]

As cash incomes fell, near famine and agricultural depres-

Table 10: Natural Increase and Population Change, Ireland, 1881-1926

Years	Natural Increase[a]	Population Change
1881-1890	+ 267,307	− 470,086
1891-1900	+ 218,985	− 245,975
1901-1910	+ 256,096	− 68,556
1911-1926	+ 216,436	− 161,666

Source: Reports of the Registrar General for Ireland, 1881-1926, in *Irish Historical Statistics*, table 43, pp. 244, 245, and 247.
[a]Births minus deaths.

sion returned. Between 1876 and 1879 the overall value of Irish agriculture fell by almost two-fifths, going from £36.5 million to £22.7 million. The credit network collapsed, and farmers' bank deposits decreased by 15 percent, dropping from £33 million to £28 million in those three years.[5] Moreover, as British agriculture mechanized, demand for Irish seasonal labor fell. By 1880 only twelve thousand workers were able to find work in Britain for part of the year. Between 1881 and 1885 their number declined to only six thousand. In those same four years, the average seasonal wage decreased from £15 to £10. Even farmers who had converted to pasturage and market agriculture were in almost as precarious a position as laborers dependent on subsistence tillage. Between 1881 and 1885 the overall value of agricultural production fell by 33 percent and that of livestock by 18 percent. By the mid-1880s prices for Irish farm products were the lowest since the Famine.[6]

These agricultural reversals had especially severe consequences among agricultural laborers in the west, the group that had maintained its population levels and subsistence economy throughout the post-Famine period. The number of evictions in the region almost tripled between 1879 and 1881, rising from 2,889 to 7,882. In some communities, the number of people on relief approached or surpassed 50 percent,[7] and starvation reappeared throughout the region.

As conditions worsened, tenant agitation for greater control over the land spread. By 1879 tenants, under the leadership of the Land League, were united into an effective political force.

Tenants made landlords, the group that controlled over 80 percent of the arable land in Ireland, the scapegoat for their growing economic troubles, and they unilaterally set limits to the
amount of rent a landlord could collect. If tenants decided a
neighbor's rent was too high, they refused to pay rents altogether. Boycotting and armed resistance to eviction spread
throughout the west and soon appeared everywhere in the country.[8]

The government responded with a series of land reforms
designed to increase the legal rights of tenants over their holdings. By the first decade of the twentieth century, government
reform had succeeded in creating a system far-reaching enough
to promote renewed agricultural prosperity outside of Ulster.
Slowly, beginning with the Land Purchase Act of 1903, landlords were coerced into selling land to tenants given purchasing
power through government loans. By 1909 much of Ireland had
been converted into a country of small peasant proprietors.[9]

As more and more tenants gained control over their holdings,
and as farmers' cooperatives and credit networks reestablished
themselves, agricultural conditions improved. As we shall see,
the cash remittances sent home by emigrant daughters and
sisters also contributed to land purchasing by former tenants.

Government land reform in the late nineteenth and early
twentieth centuries did not create true economic advance, however. Although the reforms did benefit the larger farmers, they
had little or no impact on agricultural laborers. This group had
seen only a change in masters, not a concrete improvement in
their living or working conditions.[10] In fact, despite the transfer
of more and more land to farmers in those years, Ireland remained one of the most economically backward countries in
Europe throughout the period, especially in the west.[11]

Consequently, although Parliament continued its campaign
to extend land reform in Ireland, it still faced the problem of
land fragmentation and persistent poverty in the west. Accordingly, in 1883 the Labourers' (Ireland) Act was enacted to allevi-
ate some of the worst destitution in that region. Not until 1891,
however, when the Congested Districts Board was created to
deal with areas of Ireland with per capita incomes of less than £1
10s. a year, was economic advance possible. Since these areas

were found mostly in the west, the board concentrated its efforts there. Originally, the board had jurisdiction over one-sixth of Ireland. By 1909, when land reform began to have an impact, the board controlled one-third of the country.[12]

The Congested Districts Board was one of the most successful agencies ever to deal with the land question. Acting on the premise that the only way to end continuing poverty in the west was to increase the buying power of the population there, the board created new sources of cash income in the region by encouraging domestic industries, fisheries, and trade. Further the board consolidated land holdings in the areas under its power and helped farmers realize greater profits by improving their agricultural techniques. The board also sponsored reforestation projects.[13] Nevertheless, despite its success in rejuvenating the economy in Ireland's poorest areas, the board was not able to generate enough wealth in the west to enable large numbers of tenants there to buy their holdings. In addition, despite the board's attempts to revive domestic industry in the region, the number of people employed in home production continued to fall. Ominously, while the overall number of seasonal migrants fell throughout the late nineteenth century, Connaught continued to supply 80 percent of the total.[14]

Even those farmers with something to sell did not necessarily enjoy true prosperity at the turn of the century. As one woman remembered, "Every Tuesday was Market Day. All produce, cattle, horses, and so forth were brought into the large market in the center of town. English merchants came over from England to buy, and they certainly took advantage of us. . . . Here were prize cattle, grazed on the best pastures in Ireland, fed on the best grain and then sold to crafty Englishmen. The large firkins of butter . . . went for almost nothing. . . . [They] were sold per pound in England for fancy prices. All their profits were made at the expense of the poor Irish."[15] These sentiments were echoed by a native of County Clare who recalled that his father's farm "didn't specialize in any one particular thing. You had to have a little of everything to survive."[16]

The economic stagnation of the late nineteenth and early twentieth centuries was especially injurious to women, particularly those in the west and the southwest. Despite their declining numbers in the population, women's opportunities to earn cash incomes continued to fall. After the Famine, a decrease in the supply of females, unlike that of males, did not increase either the demand for their services or their wages. Instead, men and women competed for fewer and fewer jobs. In this competition, women lost.

By the 1880s, as the effects of the economic downturn were felt throughout the country, fewer farmers could afford paid help. Moreover, as the agricultural economy shifted away from labor-intensive tillage, fewer workers were needed, and consequently, female agricultural employment declined, as displaced males replaced females in such once female jobs as dairy and poultry production. The advent of renewed prosperity after the turn of the century did little to improve farm job prospects for women either. By that time, cooperative creameries, run by men, dominated dairy production. Therefore, in spite of the high rate of female emigration after 1885, women were permanently displaced from paid agricultural work. Between 1881 and 1911, while the number of men over age twenty in the agricultural labor force fell by 15 percent, that of their female counterparts fell by over 30 percent. In those same years, the percentage of females among all agricultural workers fell from 10 to 8 percent.[17] The days of the "big stout strong lump of an agricultural Irish girl [who] can strike that hard that you'd think you'd been struck by the kick of a mule" were forever gone.[18]

Opportunities for women to earn a living outside of agriculture also grew scarcer after 1880. Home textile production, which had employed one-quarter of the female population over age fifteen in 1851, had virtually disappeared by the end of the post-Famine period, leaving thousands of women free for factory employment. Irish mills were concentrated in Belfast, however, and did not expand at a fast enough rate to absorb this new human surplus. Thus, although almost 70 percent of Belfast's linen mill workers were women, the number of women employed in Irish industry fell from 36 to 26 percent of the total industrial labor force between 1881 and 1911.[19]

Women had even less of a chance of finding an industrial job in Dublin, the only other large city in Ireland. Primarily an administrative and cutural center, Dublin had no textile industry, thereby limiting its female population to manufacturing work in small clothing, cigarette, and biscuit factories. In 1910 fewer than one in ten women there worked in industry.[20]

For the fortunate woman able to find work in Dublin, wages failed to meet even the low standards of the day. One subscriber, in a letter to the *Irish Worker* in 1911, protested the "barefaced system of white slavery . . . in the paper sorting establishment of S. Irwin and Son, 121 Upper Abbey Street . . . girls [there] are paid . . . at the rate of 2s6d to 3s a week from 8 o'clock in the morning until 7 at night . . . and are not allowed out for dinner."[21] Although other female workers were paid at slightly better rates than the exploited workers at S. Irwin and Son, most earned only between 7 and 12s. a week for long hours in Dublin's shops and offices.[22]

Working conditions, like wage levels, also brought protest from contemporary observers. According to the *Freeman's Journal* of October 6, 1913, the labor leader James Larkin urged his followers to "go to the factories and see the maimed girls, the weak and the sickly. . . . [Jacob's Biscuit Factory—a prime employer of women] had the worse sweating den in . . . Great Britain. . . . Better for Ireland that some of the industries we have . . . were destroyed and never started."[23]

Outside of the factories, the only other unskilled jobs available to women in Dublin were domestic service and prostitution. Although it paid less than 10s. a month in wages in the 1890s, life as a servant did provide a woman with room and board. Given the appalling housing conditions among the working poor in turn-of-the-century Dublin, these benefits made service a highly popular occupational choice among the city's women. By 1911 one in three Dublin women worked as a servant.[24] Nevertheless, overall female employment in domestic service fell by two-thirds between 1881 and 1911, mirroring the city's growing unemployment.

Other, less fortunate women became prostitutes. The "Monto" district of Dublin, about a quarter of a square mile in area near the center of the city, contained 132 brothels in 1868.[25] Although the number of prostitutes in the city decreased after the passage of the Criminal Law Amendment Act in 1885, which sentenced convicted brothel keepers to hard labor, more than ten thousand women were arrested for prostitution in the city between 1899 and 1914.[26] The majority were between twenty-one and thirty years old, women who presumably would have chosen safer and more respectable lines of work had they been available.

Poverty made prostitution such a fixture in city life, however, that nightly parades of young women were a common sight along Grafton and O'Connell Streets, the two principal avenues in the center of Dublin. In fact, one side of O'Connell Street was reserved for prostitutes, while respectable women strolled only along the other.[27] The prevalence of prostitution caused leaders like Larkin to point out the connection between poverty and vice. "O'Connell Street," he thundered, "was an abomination owing to the fact that girl wage slaves were driven to it under a terrible system."[28]

Although prostitution continued to be an important source of income for many of Dublin's women, the attractiveness of this employment opportunity was further reduced by the fact that the average prostitute could look forward to only five years of an active working life before disease took its toll.[29] In fact, by the turn of the century, venereal disease had become such an enormous health problem among the poor of Dublin that a special hospital for its treatment had been built.[30] Serious health risks, along with the growing sexual puritanism among the post-Famine Irish, therefore, hardly made prostitution seem a positive step toward a better life to the vast majority of women languishing in the countryside.

Dublin also did not serve as a center for other types of female employment. Although the percentage of women working in the professional and commecial sectors did increase after 1881, the number of women in these job categories was negligible in terms of the overall female work force. Consequently, as wages for women became harder and harder to find, joblessness among women over the age of twenty rose from two-thirds to three-quarters of their total number in the years between 1881 and 1911. In addition, as table 11 shows, the greatest decreases in women's employment occurred in the servant, agricultural, and industrial sectors—the key work options open to women.

Overall, Dublin's lack of female employment was only one of

Table 11: Occupational Distribution of Women, Age Twenty and Up, Ireland, 1881-1911

Occupation	1881	1891	1901	1911	%Change
Professional	20,021	25,293	27,114	33,959	+41
Servant	313,364	158,996	148,243	111,333	−64
Commercial	1,109	1,543	3,576	7,150	+84
Agricultural	84,656	83,614	81,886	58,138	−31
Industrial	199,585	186,555	176,764	134,161	−33
Unemployed	845,639	904,801	917,655	1,004,932	+16
Total	1,464,374	1,360,802	1,355,238	1,349,673	− 8

Source: Census for Ireland, 1911, cited in C.H. Oldham, "Emigration," p. 210.

the reasons the city held little attraction for girls in rural Ireland. Working and living conditions in the city resembled those associated today with the *favelas* of Rio de Janeiro and other overcrowded and undercapitalized urban areas: rampant prostitution, homeless orphans scrounging a livelihood of sorts on the street, casual labor for men.

Nor could Dublin's citizens at the turn of the century hope for a better future. Although the populations of other cities in western Europe also suffered unemployment, hunger, and disease, the economies of their cities were expanding; their privations would be temporary only. In contrast, Dublin's economy was not expanding, and expectations for better living conditions in the future could not be entertained. Indeed, the city experienced a decrease in population along with economic decline as Dublin's political importance diminished in the last half of the nineteenth century. Furthermore, by 1899 Dublin's annual death rate of 33.6 per 1,000 population outstripped even Liverpool's and, according to at least one authority, approached Calcutta's.[31] Infant mortality—at 168 deaths per 1,000 births in 1901—was Dublin's chief killer, but infectious diseases, especially tuberculosis, followed closely behind. These diseases spread quickly in Dublin's slums, where twenty-six thousand families lived in only five thousand tenements in 1914.[32] Overcrowding among the poorest third of the city's population was so severe that though officials set the minimum amount of human living space at 400 cubic feet per adult, the laws regulating dairies mandated 800 cubic feet of space for each Irish cow.[33]

These horrifying statistics help to explain the fact that although jobs for women were no more plentiful in rural than in urban Ireland in the late nineteenth and early twentieth centuries, Irish cities did not serve as meccas for the surplus rural female population in those years. In fact, rural living conditions in terms of housing and mortality improved at a much quicker pace than did those in the country's largest cities. By the turn of the twentieth century, life in Belfast and Dublin was the worst in the British Isles. Although death rates decreased in English cities in the last quarter of the nineteenth century, they increased in Irish cities in those same years. As a result, although mortality in Dublin and Belfast had been lower than in Liverpool, Manchester, and Glasgow in 1874, this was no longer true in 1900.[34] By the first decade of the twentieth century, Dublin had the highest death rate in Ireland: 24.7 for each 1,000 in the city's population, versus 17.3 for each 1,000 in the overall population. Even as late as 1936 life expectancies for both men and women were lower in cities than in rural areas. By that year life expectancy at birth was 58.2 years for males and 59.6 years for females overall, but only 53.1 years for males and 57.0 years for females born in urban areas.[35] Irish women (and men), therefore, could expect to live longer by remaining in the countryside rather than migrating to nearby cities.

Irish towns were also not magnets for rural migrants in the late nineteenth and early twentieth centuries. Opportunities for the resettlement of superfluous females living on neighboring farms were even fewer in towns than in cities. In fact, although the overall urban population did grow after 1880—reflecting Belfast's emergence as an industrial center—smaller towns of between 1,500 and 5,000 people lost population in the late nineteenth and early twentieth centuries. Furthermore, many towns actually disappeared over the course of successive censuses, making Ireland only slightly less rural in 1920 than it had been in 1880.[36]

As a result, no province was predominantly urban until 1926. Even in that year, only two provinces—Ulster, which contained

Belfast, and Leinster which contained Dublin—were more urban than rural. In 1926 rural areas still accounted for 70 percent of the population of Munster and 90 percent of the population of Connaught. Altogether, in 1926 almost 70 percent of the total Free State population and almost 50 percent of Northern Ireland's population remained in rural areas. Only in 1971 did the majority of the Republic's population live in communities of twenty or more houses.[37]

While few Irish women migrated to towns or cities in their homeland in the late nineteenth and early twentieth centuries, the vast majority of those who left the country in those years settled in urban areas abroad. By 1900, 60 percent of all the Irish in the United States lived in cities of twenty-five thousand people or more.[38] In this they followed an earlier emigrant pattern of settling in the industrial cities of Britain. Even as early as 1841, one-fifth of the Irish-born population in England, and three-fifths of the Irish-born population in Scotland, lived in cities of ten thousand people or more. By 1850 Irish emigration to both Philadelphia and London was larger than Irish migration to Dublin or any other large Irish city.[39]

In the late nineteenth and early twentieth centuries, then, the only way for an unmarried woman in rural Ireland to realize her material expectations and achieve economic independence was to emigrate to cities abroad, especially those in the United States. Although the combined impact of the Troubles and World War I increased travel to Great Britain, over 80 percent of all women emigrants between 1885 and 1920 went to the United States.[40] Furthermore, the lack of work at home and the relative ease of securing jobs as domestic servants in cities outside of Ireland fostered a mobility among Irish women unmatched by men at that time. After 1890 women outnumbered men among the Irish in England and Wales. By 1920 only seventy-three Irish-born males for each one hundred Irish-born females lived in U.S. cities.[41]

The overabundance of Irish women in foreign cities reflected how easy it was for women to obtain positions as domestic servants, an opportunity unmatched by any corresponding work for men. As a result, between two-thirds and three-quarters of all the women leaving Ireland between 1885 and the early years of the First World War chose "servant" as their occupational choice on emigration reports. During the later war years, as the number of female emigrants greatly decreased and the proportion of married women making the short trip to England increased, the percentage of women leaving the country who listed "servant" as their occupation declined. When the war ended, however, service regained its prominence in female emigrant occupational categories, as the overall number and percentage of unmarried female emigrants rose once again.[42]

The occupations of Irish women in the United States mirrored their choices on Irish emigration reports. In 1900, 54 percent of all Irish-born women in the United States were servants, according to the government. Only Swedish immigrant women, the other national group with an unmarried female majority among its emigrants in the 1890s, were more heavily represented among servants in the United States. In 1900 fully 61.5 percent of all Swedish-born women in the United States were servants. In contrast, only 21.9 percent of the English- and Welsh-born, 27.5 percent of the Scottish-born, and 9.1 percent of the Italian-born women in the United States in 1900 were listed as servants by the government.[43] To these immigrant groups, becoming a servant was shameful, to be resorted to only when there was no alternative save starvation. Unmarried Irish women, on the other hand, had long seen domestic service in households other than their own as an accepted means of earning a living. In fact, service in nearby farm households was an expected rite of passage for the daughters of Ireland's laboring poor

Nevertheless, although Irish girls accepted servanthood as a fact of life, they did not necessarily prefer it as a lifelong career. This ambivalence is dramatically evident in the words of one popular nineteenth century Irish song:

> ✳   . . . This girl was poor, she hadn't a home,
> Or a single thing she could call her own,
> Drifting about in the saddest of lives
> Doing odd jobs for other men's wives,
> As if for drudgery created,
> Begging a crust from a woman she hated.

After bemoaning the fate of the poor servant, the song continues with her saga. Leaving service for marriage to an old but wealthy man, the former servant lives to rue her decision to seek security at all costs. The song concludes with this warning:

> Is there living a girl who could grow fat
> Tied to a traveling corpse like that
> Who twice a year wouldn't find a wish
> To see what was she, flesh or fish
> But dragged the clothes about his head
> Like a wintry wind to a woman in bed?[44]

In addition, since the vast majority of the women leaving Ireland in the late nineteenth and early twentieth centuries were unmarried and traveling without their families, they were more likely to be employed outside the home than were women in any other immigrant group in the United States. In 1900, while 73 percent of all Irish-born women in the United States had jobs outside the home, only 70 percent of the Scandinavian, 62 percent of the British, and 59 percent of the Italian female immigrants held paid positions in their new country in that year.[45] For the Irish woman, emigration meant earnings. Though two-thirds of all women of working age in Ireland in 1901 had no wage-earning jobs, almost three-quarters of their sisters in the United States in 1900 were earning independent livelihoods.

High literacy rates among Irish female emigrants also helped these young women adjust to their new urban lives. Despite their status as unskilled servants, Irish women settling in the United States in the late nineteenth and early twentieth centuries were more literate than were either their counterparts at home or the men and women in most other immigrant groups. Although only 86 percent of all the Irish and only 72 percent of the population of Connaught over age five could read and write in 1901, 97.4 percent of Irish immigrants to the United States between 1899 and 1910 (more than half of whom were women from the west and southwest) could read and write in English. In fact, of the forty national groups counted by the U. S. government, only Scandinavian, British, Bohemian, and Moravian immigrants had higher literacy rates than did the Irish. Conversely, only one-quarter of the Jewish and only one-half of the southern Italian immigrants in those years were literate.[46]

High levels of both female literacy and employment abroad among Irish women during this period combined in the form of the all-important "letter from America." Women's work after emigration remained vital to the family economy and often made the difference between survival and destitution. By the 1890s over $5 million a year in the form of cash remittances sent by young women overseas maintained their families' small, obsolete farms in rural Connaught and Munster.[47] Farmers hoped to be "as rich as two Yankee letters," and a woman remembered her childhood in the 1890s when "our horse died . . . that was a great loss in those days . . . an American letter [came] from Aunt Gracie, my father's sister. . . . In the letter was £20 . . . to buy a new horse."[48]

In addition to providing livestock purchase funds, cash donations from sisters and daughters abroad also provided the bulk of the passage money for their siblings. According to another beneficiary of his sister' largesse, "[My family] . . . were farmers . . . with six children . . . and no means of income other than small farming. . . . My oldest sister got a chance to come to America . . . and thereafter followed at least one of us every year."[49] In fact, of all steerage passengers leaving Ireland for the United States between 1904 (the first year this information was included on Irish emigration reports) and the outbreak of war in 1914 (when this practice was discontinued), over one-third had had their passage prepaid in the United States. The importance of female remittances in financing the emigration of brothers and sisters is reinforced by U. S. immigration documents. According to these records, almost two-fifths of all the Irish entering the country between 1908 and 1910 had had their passage paid by a relative.[50]

By emigrating to foreign cities, Irish women also continued the practice of earning enough income to preserve the traditional family organization at home. As one brother recalled, "[My sister] sent me pants, a sweater, and a pair of pants for my Communion." Later, she sent him a pair of shoes with her earnings. "I was eleven years old before I wore shoes," he remembered. In all, "my older sister . . . [sent money home] every week. . . . And it was then that things started to pick up."[51] Ironically, however, the successful adaptation of these women to urban society abroad helped maintain obsolete patterns of life in rural Ireland that would have disappeared, albeit at a tremendous human cost, without that financial support. The most expendable group in post-Famine Ireland—dependent daughters and sisters—became the saviors of a society that could not have remained intact save by their emigration and their remittances.

Nevertheless, although the movement of young women out of Ireland can be seen as a delaying tactic, both preserving out-of-date family work patterns and preventing the need for further economic change, it also allowed these women to achieve an independent adult status, something they could not have done at home. The low incidence of return among these emigrants (only 2.1 percent of all Irish immigrants to the United States between 1899 and 1910 returned to Ireland),[52] indicates that these women were pulled as much as pushed from their rural homes by the promise of an independent and productive life in the far more dynamic environment of foreign cities.

Emigration from Ireland can be seen as a long-term process of urbanizing a rural population. Great Britain and especially the United States offered expanding industrial centers and a growing middle class in need of servants. As a result, young women left their homes to seek jobs that were not available in their own country, and at the same time Ireland's industrial and urban development was severely retarded because so much of its potentially vast supply of cheap labor had gone abroad. Emigration also decreased demand for Irish manufactured goods, thereby hindering the expansion of Irish towns. Since the population fell by half between 1845 and 1920, mass consumption could only gain a toehold in Ireland in the late nineteenth and early twentieth centuries, despite the gradual rise in real incomes. High female emigration in those years also had an indirect effect on the failure of Irish industry to expand in the course of these years. Since Ireland lost the better part of a generation of potential mothers, the mass consumer society needed in a healthy industrial economy could not be born. Consequently, the mass migration of young women out of Ireland reinforced the pattern of Irish economic and social stagnation.

CHAPTER FIVE

Irish Women in America
1880-1920

The mass migration of women described here may first appear to be a passive retreat of superfluous females from inhospitable circumstances. Closer inspection of their emigration, however, reveals that these women actively chose to abandon diminished lives at home and to embrace adventure abroad while seeking jobs, husbands, and an independent adult status. Unlike those who remained "old girls" on their parents' or siblings' farms, the thousands of young, unmarried women who left the country between 1885 and 1920 rejected dependency and chose emigration instead.

The persistence of such a uniform emigrant generation after 1885 can be attributed to Ireland's failure to create an urban and industrial culture after the Famine. The inhibiting social, demographic, and economic constraints placed on women promoted overall economic recovery but, at the same time, also prevented women from achieving an adult status as wives and wage earners within the still agricultural world of rural Ireland. These dispossessed women looked abroad for the opportunity to fulfill their social and economic aspirations. But they did not simply follow in the footsteps of earlier female emigrants. Although Ireland had not urbanized or industrialized in the course of the nineteenth century, it had not retained its traditional culture either. Even before the Famine, individualistic patterns of early and universal marriage and population growth had already begun to alter rural life. After the Famine, when delayed and restricted marriage became the norm everywhere in the country, emigration became the only means for men and women alike to attain the modern, urban goals of early marriage and economic independence.

Thus, the young women who left Ireland after 1885 had already experienced significant changes in their traditional expectations. As a result, although they were willing after their emigration to work in nonindustrial jobs such as domestic service and to remain within the family economy, they also expected to earn independent incomes, marry, and reproduce—all individualistic aspects of the thwarted modernization of Irish life in the first half of the nineteenth century.

The emigration of young women out of Ireland did not represent a radical break with Irish culture. Rather, it represented a rejection of the celibacy and unemployment that faced them in post-Famine Ireland. Irish-born women in foreign cities sought jobs such as domestic service that were extensions of their duties in rural Ireland and did not enter the industrial work force in large numbers. In addition, once they settled in the United States, they returned to the freer marriage patterns of pre-Famine Ireland, abandoning the constraints that had bound them at home. They married fellow Irish emigrants, left the outside workplace, and entered the sphere of home and family, as their ancestors had for generations before the Famine. Once married, they retained the high fertility of their rural Irish sisters. By emigrating, Irish women were able to regain their adult status as cash producers and/or as wives within the family economy, something they could no longer do in rural Ireland.

As we have seen, the average rate of marriage dropped and the average age of marriage rose in Ireland throughout the late nineteenth and early twentieth centuries. Only by emigrating could women regain the opportunity to marry and reproduce like their mothers and grandmothers (or, in the case of those in the west and the southwest, like their older sisters). Marriage ages among the Irish in foreign cities, therefore, resembled those of the pre-Famine rather than post-Famine Ireland.

Even as early as the 1850s, Irish-born women in London were marrying at significantly lower ages than were rural Irish women.[1] By moving to London, rural Irish men and women could lower their probable age at marriage by three years to age twenty-eight for men and age twenty-six for women. Throughout the 1850s the average age at marriage for both men and women continued to fall among the Irish abroad while it remained high in rural Ireland. In 1861 the average marriage age for the London Irish was only twenty-six for men and twenty-four for women. By that year the Irish-born in London were even marrying at younger ages than were their English counterparts, something that had not been true ten years before. By the midnineteenth century, then, the Irish in London had returned to the pre-Famine practice of early and universal marriage.

The Irish in the United States followed the marriage practices of their London counterparts. As one daughter of Irish-born parents recalled, "The Irish didn't marry . . . young . . . in Ireland [but] . . . when they came [to the United States] they marr[ied] at age twenty on."[2] The Irish in the United States, like those in London, also tended to marry other Irish. In fact, the almost universal distaste among the Irish for intermarriage with other groups was justified on both religious and cultural grounds. As one female immigrant from Roscommon insisted, "I would like [my children] to marry someone of the same faith." Another woman, who had left Ireland in the early twentieth century, echoed this sentiment. "I firmly disapprove of the Irish marrying people of other nationalities and, above all, of different religions," she maintained.[3]

Although intermarriage was condemned for religious reasons, cultural factors appear to have been an even more important reason for the endogamy among the Irish in the United States. The few who broke with convention met with pity and scorn. "My daughters are both married to Italian fellows . . . I am sorry to admit," confessed one mother who had emigrated from County Kerry in 1882. Another woman who had left Ireland at the turn of the century bemoaned the fact that her "cousin married a Hungarian. Poor fellow, when he gets with a bunch of Irish men he sure seems a misfit." Since both Italians and Hungarians shared the Roman Catholicism of the Irish, religion does not seem to have been as important as nationality in the choice of a spouse. Even fellow Celts of other nationalities were considered improper marriage partners. "I don't like all these marriages with foreigners," complained a son of a woman who had left Ireland in 1902. "My sister married a Scotchman and that's bad enough." The prevailing attitude toward the selection of a spouse among the Irish in the United States was summed up by a woman who had arrived there in the early years of the twentieth century. "The Irish are intellectual, thrifty, witty, and usually fair of looks," she explained. "So why not marry [an Irishman] and make a better race?"[4]

Not only did most Irish in the United States marry other Irish, they often married those from the same area of Ireland. Accordingly, "about three months [after my arrival in the United States], I made the acquaintance of a boy from back home," a woman remembered. "After a six months courtship, we married." A man recalled that "I was [in the United States] a year when I met my first wife. She was from my hometown [of Galway]."[5]

Irish immigrants in the United States also revived the practice of early and universal marriage. Although one man insisted that "if I [can]not find a [bride] of my own nationality and religion, I [will] stay single," few Irish in the United States were unable to meet a prospective marriage partner. "Every Sunday night," remembered a woman who left County Clare in 1879, "a crowd of us [had] a party at [a] friend's house, maybe a dance. . . . It was at one of those dances . . . that I met my husband. I was then eighteen and a year later we married." A male immigrant recalled that "during my fifth year here, I married . . . [an] Irish girl from Dublin. She had been here two years when we married. . . . I met her at a wedding." "We attended many social activities held by Irish immigrants," an Irish-born woman explained. "At one of these I met my husband . . . an immigrant from Roscommon. . . . Only eight years after I came [to the United States], I was married."[6]

After their emigration, Irish females maintained the high marital fertility of their predecessors and contemporaries at home. Biology remained destiny, and childbearing and child-rearing took up a large part of married women's lives, just as they had for generations. In 1901 fully 30 percent of all Irish women aged fifteen to forty-four gave birth, and the 1,049,413 women of fertile age in Ireland in that year were surrounded by 1,353,202 children under age fourteen.[7] Their sisters in the United States demonstrated similar fertility patterns. In 1920, while three-quarters of all Irish-born women giving birth in the United States had done so at least once before, only two-thirds of their American-born counterparts could make the same claim. Furthermore, Irish-born mothers had more children overall than did their American-born neighbors. For instance, in 1920 over half of the women giving birth in the Irish-American community had already had at least three other children; only 45 percent of their American-born contemporaries had given birth so often. As a result of such high fertility, as early as 1900 the average Irish-American family was larger by one than the average American family.[8] As one daughter of an Irish-born mother saw it, "they went to work and married and then became mothers."[9]

Mary Ann Donovan's life mirrored that of other Irish women of her generation.[10] Soon after her arrival in the United States, she found work as a presser of fancy shirts in Mr. Spiney's laundry near her sister's home in Lynn, Massachusetts. Eight years later, at the age of twenty-four, she married Harry Nolan, a fellow immigrant from Cork. Thenceforward, Mary Ann's day-to-day life increasingly involved taking care of her large family. Altogether, she became the mother of six sons and three daughters. The first child, John, was born in 1898, when Mary Ann was twenty-six, two years after her marriage and ten years after her arrival in the United States. Her last child, Helen, was born in 1916. Mary Ann had given birth every other year for eighteen years by the time she reached her forty-fourth birthday on Saint Patrick's Day, 1916.

The patterns of women's work after emigration varied with their marital status, but both unmarried and married women abroad sought paid employment. As we have seen, Irish women in the United States were vital to their families' economic survival, just as women had been in traditional Irish life.

Unmarried Irish women quickly found work in American cities, earned independent incomes, and participated in the family economy by supporting themselves, saving for their own and their sisters' dowries, sending cash remittances back to Ireland to maintain the family farm, and financing the emigration of siblings. Irish immigrant females rarely joined the industrial work force in their new urban environments, however, despite their success in the outside workplace. In fact, Irish-born

Table 12: Female Employment Percentages in Selected Occupations, by Birth, United States, 1900

Occupation	Native-Born	All Foreign-Born	Irish-Born
Service	18.2	37.8	54.0
Needle trades	14.4	13.6	7.5
Textiles	5.1	10.0	7.4
Clerical	6.5	2.3	1.2
Sales	3.2	2.0	1.2
Teachers	10.8	2.0	1.5

Source: Census for the United States, U.S. Congress, Senate, *Reports of the Immigration Commission:* pp. 804-20.

women were far less likely to enter factory work than were women of other immigrant groups, as can be seen in table 12. Instead, Irish-born women in the United States chose jobs that were extensions of their traditional domestic skills. As we have seen, over one half of all the Irish women in the United States in the late nineteenth and early twentieth centuries worked as domestic servants.

An explanation of the popularity of domestic service among Irish women in the United States was offered by a servant who had left Roscommon in 1917. "Being the daughter of farmers," she commented, "[I was] . . . suited to this type of work. [My] mother . . . needed . . . help . . . for there were so many to cook for. . . . This is . . . how [I] learned to cook." She continued, "I liked [my job] as I met girls from my country all in the employ of families, either as cooks or waitresses." Occupational mobility within the ranks of house servants was another advantage to the job, according to many immigrant women. As one recalled with pride, "I was the head cook . . . the number one cook in the house." Another asserted, "I was considered a first class pastry and regular cook."[11]

Despite its attractions, service could be a dreary life. "I worked in New York for a number of years. . . . I did not have much of a good time when I was there. We had our half-days off but I only attended . . . church [or took] my walks in the parks. I was not one for the high life in the city," said one former servant, speaking of the loneliness of her first years in the United States. The labor itself was also arduous. "[I worked] as a house-worker—in those days housework meant cooking, cleaning the house and the laundry—we had to wash each piece separately on the wash board," recalled another.[12]

Serious as these drawbacks were, however, domestic service provided an important transition from rural to urban life for the majority of Irish women in the United States at this time. "After coming to America and working [as a domestic servant] for about a year . . . I got married," remembered one woman born in County Clare. A son of an immigrant mother recalled, "When mother was married, she gave up her position as house-keeper. . . . In those days, the girls stayed with [a] family until they were married." Since service was seen as only a temporary stage in life, its hardships could be easily overlooked. Service could also be lucrative. The same son remembered that her employers "gave my mother a dozen coin silver spoons for her wedding present." One well-adjusted servant enjoyed her in-come. "[I] saved good portions of [my] earnings. . . . as I received $65 per month, I had plenty."[13]

After marriage, Irish-born wives abroad returned to the eco-nomic as well as the demographic behavior of their pre-Famine forebears, something they could not have done in the changed economy of late nineteenth- and early twentieth-century Ire-land. Although "when women married, they stayed home,"[14] Irish-born wives in the United States continued to earn cash from a variety of tasks, such as taking in laundry or lodgers, just like their pre-Famine antecendents. Fifteen percent of all Irish-American households in 1900 earned income from an average of two lodgers housed in each. Widows also continued to contribute to the family economy. As one woman remembered, "My father . . . drowned . . . [leaving] . . . my mother . . . a widow with four children. The small insurance policy went to cover funeral ex-penses only. Mother did all sorts of work to raise the family. She did domestic nursing . . . she ran a boarding house and had work from Warner's corset factory brought to the house. She did pretty well, and made enough money to build the house we are now living in. When she died, there was no mortgage on the house, and all the children had been well educated."[15]

In fact, the income earned by wives in their homes helped the Irish rank ninth in home ownership out of a total of thirty-seven national groups enumerated by the U. S. government in 1900. In that year 30 percent of all Irish-American families lived in their own homes.[16] Home ownership among the Irish in the United States was as dependent on the earnings of the wife as rent payments had been in Ireland in the first half of the nineteenth century. The traditional housewarmings that marked the entrance of a neighbor into the home-owning class, independent of the landlord, had been a cause of major celebration in rural Ireland and remained a joyous community occasion among the Irish in the United States. For instance, Mary Ann Donovan Nolan threw just such a party on the occasion of her family's move into their first nonrented American home. Local musicians brought their fiddles, and sandwiches, cake, and ice cream (Prohibition prevented the free flow of whiskey) enlivened the neighborhood's christening of Mary Ann's new home and new status.

The traditional emphasis on the wife as mother was also reinforced by the wage-earning patterns in immigrant families over time. Although most wives worked outside the home before marriage and continued to generate family income by their work within the home after marriage, they left the paid work force as soon as their children were old enough to earn money. As a result, only 6 percent of all Irish-born female workers in 1900 were over age forty-five, the age at which most mothers had children in their late teens. In contrast, fully 40 percent of all Irish-born male workers in that year were over age forty-five.[17]

Thus, while one-third of Irish-American families received income from either the direct wages of the wife or from her indirect wages collected from boarders and lodgers, over two-fifths of these families also enjoyed income from the wages earned by unmarried children—daughters and sons alike.[18] Children were once again economic assets, just as they had been before the Famine. As one daughter of Irish-born immigrants remembered, "[My father's job] kept us going . . . And then I had a brother in the police force. He kept us going also. And the rest [of my brothers] worked whenever they could find a job . . . My mother never worked. She had so much to do around [the house]

Table 13: School Attendance Percentages among Children Aged Six to Sixteen, by Nativity of Father, United States, 1900

	Male	Female	Total
American-born	90.9	90.5	90.7
All foreign-born	83.9	83.5	83.7
Irish-born	89.6	91.4	90.5

Source: Census for the United States, U.S. Congress Senate, *Report of the Immigration Commission: Abstracts,* pp. 470, 471.

. . . I was training to be a nurse . . . [I was] paid five dollars a month." [19]

Nevertheless, as in Ireland, the Irish in the United States insisted on sending their children to school. In fact, school attendance among children with Irish-born parents equaled that of children with American-born parents and exceeded that of most other immigrant groups. These differences are even more telling when the percentages of girls aged six to sixteen in school are considered. As can be seen in table 13, school attendance among girls with Irish-born fathers surpassed not only that of their brothers but also that of the daughters of either American-born or other foreign-born fathers. This pattern reflects the traditional Irish view that education was as important to a girl's upbringing as to a boy's.

As a result of the relatively extensive education received by daughters in Irish-American families, job mobility among second-generation Irish women in the United States far exceeded that of most other national groups, as can be seen in table 14. For instance, only Scandinavian women outnumbered Irish women among foreign-born domestic servants in American cities. In the second generation, however, over one-half of Scandinavian daughters remained in domestic service, but only one-quarter of their Irish counterparts continued to be servants. Second generation Irish-American women also entered the professions in significant numbers.

As table 14 demonstrates, while less than 4 percent of all Irish-born women in the United States in 1900 were white collar workers, over 14 percent of their second generation counterparts

Table 14: Female Employment Percentages in Selected Occupations, by Nativity, United States, 1900

Occupation	Born Abroad			Born in the U.S.		
	Irish	Scandi-navian[a]	Other	Irish	Scandi-navian[a]	Other
Professional	3.3	3.2	5.7	14.1	11.4	13.4
Service	70.4	68.0	39.7	25.1	52.4	26.0
Manufacing	20.1	16.8	45.8	45.4	22.3	43.7
Agriculture	2.8	8.9	4.6	1.4	2.6	4.4

Source: Census for the United States, U.S. Congress, Senate, Reports of the Immigration Commission: Abstracts, table 21B, pp. 470, 471.
[a]Includes Sweden, Norway, and Denmark.

in that year were teachers, bookkeepers, accountants, and typists. "[Teaching] had status," according to one teacher, the daughter of Irish-born parents. "[You were] looked up to . . . like a doctor." Furthermore, as Irish-American women acclimated themselves to their new urban environments, their participation in the industrial work force increased. The teacher continued, "Some [women] worked as maids, . . . that wasn't looked up to)—[it] was kind of degrading. They were better off to go to work in a factory."[20]

Many daughters of immigrant Irish parents appear to have agreed. While only one-fifth of Irish-born female workers in 1900 earned their living from manufacturing, over two-fifths of all second-generation Irish women in that year worked in factories. Both first- and second-generation Irish women in the United States were, however, the least represented among seventeen national groups in the agricultural work force. Having once escaped the farm, Irish women and their daughters had no desire to return to it.

Once again, Mary Ann Donovan Nolan's experiences reflect the ideals of her generation. Despite financial hardship, she insisted that each of her children receive as much education as possible. Although she was a widow before her four youngest children had reached the age of twenty, five of her nine children, including all of her three daughters, went on to higher education, becoming teachers, bookkeepers, and engineers.

Although the lives of Irish women in the United States have been well-documented, the following survey of their activities after emigration will demonstrate that female emigration from Ireland in the late nineteenth and early twentieth centuries resulted in something of a paradox. Although emigration liberated a generation from a life of celibate dependency on family farms, it did not liberate them from their traditional domestic responsibilities. Nevertheless, emigration did allow women to regain their social and economic equality as wives within the family economy, as we have seen, and it enabled the daughters of these women to establish new paths unheard of in rural Ireland, as we are beginning to see.

Even though service was the primary means for an Irish woman to gain a toehold in the American economy, not all servants enjoyed their employment. Poor working and living conditions as well as low pay contributed to this dissatisfaction, but the disdain felt by many native-born Americans for the Irish was also a major factor in a servant's dislike of her work. Young Irish women were held in low esteem by both their employers and their sister employees. Employers sought "neat, tidy English girl[s]" or "respectable Protestant girl[s]." [21] As one co-worker observed in 1890, "A great many very ignorant girls can get housework to do, and a girl who has been used to the neatness and the refinement of a good home does not like to room with a girl who has just come from Ireland and does not know what neatness means." [22]

Moreover, as a contemporary study of domestic service in the 1880s and 1890s conclded, "the servility of manner demanded . . . of all domestics is an anomaly in a country where there is no enforced recognition of social and political superiors." Therefore, according to the testimony collected by the study, servants found their station objectionable because "no one likes to be called a 'hired girl,'" and since "domestics are not admitted into any society, [they] are often for want of a little pleasure driven to seek it in company that is often coarse and vulgar." [23]

Turnover among servants was rapid, and few viewed service as a permanent way of life. Therefore, although the demand for servants remained high, the Boston Young Women's Christian Association's domestic employment bureau was able to fill only

1,753 out of the 2,120 requests for servants it received in 1890. An association committee, noting the discrepancy between the number of positions offered and the number of positions filled, wrote, "The demand [for servants] is great in the city, but more so in the suburbs and country. It is very difficult to find a woman willing to take service in a family living out of sight of the Boston Common."[24] Once Irish girls had left their subservient positions in the Irish countryside, they had no desire to return to them across the water.

Irish women did return to their formerly active place in public life after emigration, however. Irish-American women were overrepresented among the leaders of the American labor movement despite their relatively low rate of participation in the industrial labor force. As early as 1868 Kate Mullany had organized her sister laundry workers in Troy, New York, into a "Laundry Union and Co-Operative Collar Company" for the purpose of alleviating intolerable working conditions and increasing worker profits. In 1885 the Knights of Labor, then the largest union in the United States, elected Leonora Barry, a native of Ireland, to its recently formed Committee on Women's Work. A widowed mother and a former hosiery worker, Barry organized women in occupations ranging from housekeeping to factory work on a nationwide scale. Although Barry retired from public life when she remarried in 1890 (thereby following the traditional Irish pattern), her place in the labor movement was soon filled by a succession of second generation Irish-American women. In 1892 Mary Kenny O'Sullivan became the American Federation of Labor's first female organizer. Leonora O'Reilly established the New York chapter of the Women's Trade Union League in 1904, a year after Agnes Nestor was elected president of the International Glove Workers Union. By 1912 the International Brotherhood of the Electrical Workers had chosen Julia O'Connor to lead its telephone operators department. Perhaps the most famous second-generation Irish-American woman in the American labor movement in the early twentieth century was Elizabeth Gurley Flynn, a leader of the Industrial Workers of the World, the radical labor organization Irish-born Mother Mary Harris Jones had helped establish in 1905.[25]

Public school teachers, many of whom were daughters of Irish female emigrants, were organized by leaders such as Kate Kennedy in San Francisco, Margaret Haley and Catherine Goggins in Chicago, and Kate Hogan, Anna McAuliffe, Ellen O'Brien, and Annie Moriarty in New York City.[26] Arguing that women teachers deserved equal pay for equal work, each of these activists held the traditional Irish view that a woman's work was as important as a man's for the family's economic survival.

Irish-American women were also active in the cause of Irish independence, a political movement of great importance to the Irish both at home and abroad in the late nineteenth and early twentieth centuries. One such woman, Mary Keena, organized the American Association for the Recognition of the Irish Republic for the purpose of raising funds for and public interest in the revolutionary movement in Ireland. While picketing the British embassy in Washington, D.C., Keena was asked why she had become an activist for the Irish Nationalist cause. She replied, "It has been a hard, hard duty, but as I cannot shoulder a gun, I will at least let our people know what the horrors of British militarism are."[27]

Irish-American women did not ignore American politics either. Mary Donovan Hapgood was as determined a political activist as Keena. Called the "Joan of Arc of the Labor Movement" by Upton Sinclair, Hapgood joined the Socialist party and was elected recording secretary of the Sacco-Vanzetti Defense Committee; she named her daughter Barta after Bartolomeo Vanzetti. As the Socialist party candidate in 1928, she was the first woman ever nominated for governor in Massachusetts.[28]

Other Irish-American women joined the Ancient Order of Hibernians, the largest Irish-American cultural and social welfare organization outside of the Catholic church, when its Ladies' Auxiliary was chartered in 1890. In a speech given at the AOH convention in that year, a Miss Laughlin calmed male fears about female membership by stating, "now, by our presence here, we do not want . . . to be speechmakers, or . . . political speakers . . . we are not the 'New Woman,' but women who have good Irish mothers who taught them to cook, to sew, to wash, to iron, and to get a good square meal for their husbands." She concluded her talk, however, with a thinly veiled announcement that Irish-American women would no longer be content to remain in the background. "The time, has almost arrived," McLaughlin told her audience, "when women and men can stand on equal ground . . ."[29]

Like their male counterparts, Auxiliary members were active supporters of revolution in Ireland, and like Mary Keena, the Ladies raised money for the establishment of the new Irish Republic. For instance, in 1892, at the age of twenty, Mary Ann Donovan was elected charter president of the Lynn, Massachusetts, chapter of the Ladies' Auxiliary of the AOH. Later, she became the first vice president of the Essex County Auxiliary. Eventually, she held statewide office in this national organization. Even after her marriage, she continued representing her constituents at state and national AOH conventions.

In her capacity as an AOH leader, Nolan came into close contact with both Irish Nationalist and American political leaders. She greeted many of the most important people in the Nationalist movement when they visited the heavily Irish industrial city that was her home. On one occasion, she accompanied Maud Gonne in the limousine that led a massive AOH Nationalist parade through the streets of Lynn. She also sold Irish Republican war bonds door to door. Although the Irish Republic did not yet exist, her faith in its inevitability prompted many an otherwise skeptical Irish-American to buy a bond with hard-earned cash. As her neighbor John Quigley explained, "If Mary Ann Nolan says these bonds are good, then they are good no matter what England has to say about it."[30]

Besides raising money for the establishment of the new Irish Republic, the Auxiliary also ran Saturday night dances that were among the most important social events in Irish-American communities.[31] While local bands such as Joe O'Leary's Irish Minstrels played traditional Irish reels and more recent popular songs written by Irish-American composers, the dances provided a meeting place for "greenhorns" and their more sophisticated American cousins. The AOH hall, festooned with portraits of American patriots besting the British in the Revolutionary War and of Irish patriots besting the British at various times throughout Irish history, was as important as the church as a community focal point in American cities with large Irish populations. There, talk of American politics, Irish rebellion, romance, and other local gossip united the Irish in the United States just as the fairs and the village celebrations had enlivened traditional Irish life. Although the Ladies' Auxiliary was dependent on the larger male organization, participation in its many activities brought housebound wives, widows, and servant girls into the wider world of public Irish America.

Irish women in the United States also returned to their traditional level of formal and informal interaction with other women by recreating the female networks that had vanished in the gloomy world of post-Famine Irish life. Although Irish women lagged behind other female immigrants in forming women's organizations (as late as 1921 there were few secular national organizations for Irish women outside of the Ladies' Auxiliary of the AOH),[32] this lack of formal organization did not prevent them from restoring the tradition of banding together for communal self-help. In addition, although one daughter of Irish immigrants recalled that "we had no clubs for ladies until later," [33] Irish-American women showed no reluctance to participate in sexually integrated labor unions, political groups, and recreational activities.

Perhaps the single most important outlet for women in Irish-American communities was the church. In fact, Irish women in the United States were as generous to the church as they were to their families back in Ireland. Many an American parish's church and school building program was successfully financed by the contributions of female immigrants. Irish-American women were also integral to the formation of women's sodalities, benevolent associations, temperance unions, and other organizations vital to a parish's social and spiritual life.[34] As one second-generation Irish-American woman in New Britain, Connecticut, recalled, "the Church used to help you if you were in dire need. We had a Diocesan Bureau [run by] Miss Marony [who] would see to it if any family needed care." [35] Moreover, as the Irish in the United States grew more prosperous, Irish-American women were able to expand their local activities. For instance, in 1920 a Council of Catholic Women was organized in Bridgeport, Connecticut, as an auxiliary to the male-dominated Charitable Bureau of the Bridgeport diocese. The founding

members were all Irish-American women.[36] In Hartford, Connecticut, the Ladies of Charity was organized to raise money for
a local Catholic hospital. The Ladies had units in parishes
throughout the Hartford area where "women [met] regularly to
sew apparel for patients . . . [and] make bandages and surgical
dressings." The Ladies, again dominated by Irish-American
women, also provided an active social life for members. "The
annual program . . . includes dances, bridge parties, dinners,
theater parties, garden parties and lectures," wrote an observer.
"The Annual Charity Ball was for many years a distinctive
social function for Hartford's Social Elite," he continued, adding
that these endeavors were "well supported by the more prosperous [Irish] Catholic women of the city and suburbs."[37]

Furthermore, although nuns represented only a tiny minority of all women in both Ireland and Irish-America, their activities were crucial to the social welfare of Irish immigrants in
the United States. Nuns staffed parochial schools and Catholic
colleges, ran hospitals, and provided homes for unwed mothers
and deserted wives. While Irish-American priests oversaw the
spiritual welfare of their flocks, Irish-American nuns saw to
their physical as well as their spiritual well-being. But although
it was widely noted that the Irish dominated the American
Catholic church by the late nineteenth century, the role of Irish
women—both lay and religious—in this phenomenon received
very little attention.[38]

By 1925, however, Irish-American women had become successful enough to warrant notice in some previously all-male
circles. For instance, in that year the *Journal* of the American
Irish Historical Society published an article on "American Irish
Women 'Firsts.'"[39] Included were brief profiles of several Irish-
American women who had achieved prominence in conven-
tional politics and law by the early twentieth century. Women
such as the following were recognized: Mae Nolan of San Francisco, the second woman elected to the House of Represen-
tatives; Mary Norton of New Jersey, the first woman elected to
the House from an eastern state; Helen McCormick, the first
female assistant district attorney in the western hemisphere;
and Jean Norris, the first female magistrate of the state of New
York. The article continued by listing the perhaps even more

impressive accomplishments of women actually born in Ireland, including Ellen O'Grady, a native of Limerick and a mother of five, the first deputy police commissioner in the United States; and Mary O'Toole, born in County Carlow, the first woman judge on the bench of the Municipal Court of Washington, D.C.

Despite this acknowledgment of Irish-American women's accomplishments, the attitudes toward women held by most Irish-American men continued to reflect the ideal of feminine subservience of post-Famine Ireland. For instance, although Terrence Powderly, himself the son of an Irish female immigrant as well as the leader of the Knights of Labor, encouraged women to participate in the Knights' activities, he "wished it was not necessary for women to learn any trade but that of domestic duties, as I believe it was intended that the man should be the breadwinner."[40] Powderly's sentiments were echoed throughout male Irish-America. "I do believe the husband should be the provider for the family," contended one man who had left County Cork for the United States in 1894.[41]

Another man, also a native of County Cork, agreed. "I do not approve of married women out in the . . . world," he declared. A compatriot from County Clare concurred, insisting that "married women . . . belong in the home." A Galway native, who had arrived in the United States in 1900, also rejected the idea of married women's working outside the home. "I detest thoughts of married women in the business world," he maintained. A native of County Sligo concluded that "women should not work after marriage . . . their place is in the home."[42]

Irish women in the United States, however, had returned to the freer female ideal of pre-Famine Ireland. Even according to the very same men just quoted, married women's work was objectionable more on economic than social grounds, and they did not disapprove of unmarried women's working outside the home. As one explained, married women "work in offices or teaching and take the jobs of men and single girls." Another, who also believed that married women should remain within the home, admitted that "my wife and I talk over financial matters together . . . we live our lives very similarly to that we led in Ireland."[43]

Nevertheless, Irish women in the United States had regained

the freedom that women had had in pre-Famine Ireland. By emigrating, Irish women had perforce abandoned the post-Famine dependency thrust upon them by the weight of demographic and economic change, even if the attitudes of their male counterparts had not kept pace. As one native of Ireland conceded, "My wife is rather a boss . . . I told her she must have some ancestors in the Prussian army. She sure can give orders." [44]

Conclusion:
"Ourselves Alone"

The mass exodus of women from Ireland between 1885 and 1920 cannot be explained by the accepted interpretations of European female emigration in those years. Since Irish women emigrated independently of husbands or fathers, their emigration was not a passive carrying of traditional family culture across the Atlantic in the wake of male relatives. Furthermore, unlike their counterparts in other national groups, the women who left Ireland in the late nineteenth and early twentieth centuries were the successors to a generation of sustained female emigration. Well before the 1880s, the precedent for the migration of unmarried women, traveling alone to foreign cities, had been established.

Therefore, although the emigration of single women independently from parents or husbands was an anomaly in the history of overall European emigration, it was not an anomaly in the history of Irish emigration. Throughout the nineteenth century, Irish emigration patterns had always reflected the demographic and conomic displacement of varying groups within the population. By 1885 dispossessed women in the west and the southwest became the last of these groups to leave Ireland in large enough numbers to dominate overall emigration totals. Moreover, like many of their predecessors, female emigrants between 1885 and 1920 sought to regain their pre-Famine status as wives and economic partners within the family, something they could no longer do in the changed world of post-Famine Irish life.

Unlike other European female emigrants, the single women who left Ireland after 1880 were not abandoning traditional culture or carrying an intact traditional culture abroad. Rather, their journey to urban America represented a recovery of an

opportunity once lost. The legions of young women leaving rural
Ireland in the late nineteenth and early twentieth centuries
were discarding their newly subservient and marginal positions
in their home communities, not their traditional expectations.
Although the specifics of her life after emigration may not have
been typical, Irish-born movie actress Maureen O'Hara had
experiences in the United States that mirrored those of many
women in her generation. As her friend, also an emigrant from
Ireland, recalled, "she had six . . . or seven . . . children . . . she
led a very home life. In many ways, the way she would have lived
in Ireland."[1]

Since women had occupied a position of strength in pre-
Famine rural life, their return to earlier patterns of female
behavior after emigration was not a backward step. In fact, the
reappearance of pre-Famine female roles within the Irish-
American family enabled emigrant women and their daughters
to emerge as active forces in their new communities. Their
emigration signified their active choice to regain lost social and
economic power.

The self-assertion of these Irish female emigrants was also
underscored by the the fact that while the emigration of females
in other national groups was financed and led by male relatives,
the migration of Irish women was financed and led by female
relatives. The female network that had been lost in the post-
Famine reorganization of Irish life was restored to its former
importance by the very nature of emigration in those years.
Since female emigrants were the primary suppliers of cash
remittances to their families in rural Ireland, the sustained
migration of young women from these families created continuous moral and financial support for the subsequent migration of
their siblings, nieces, nephews, and cousins. Many of the young
women leaving Ireland could have echoed the statement made
by this young woman, born in County Clare. "My sister in [the
United States]," she explained, "sent me the money to come to
America."[2]

Furthermore, although most of the young women leaving
Ireland lacked the protection and companionship of a husband
on their journey, they were able to emigrate independently of
male domination. Once established abroad, they freely chose

when and whom to marry, just as they had before the Famine. In this they were able to reassert their lost freedom in the choice of their adult demographic and economic roles. Had they stayed at home, these women would have lived celibate and unproductive lives in a stagnant economy.

Irish women continued to emigrate into the twentieth century despite occasionally discouraging reports from the United States, such as this December 1913 complaint that "times are pretty hard in America at present. Food is high and work is slack . . . there will be a lot of people who can't afford to have such a merry Christmas in the Land of the Free." [3] Since their status at home remained low and the prospects for its improvement dim, women realized that their liberation required emigration. The long tradition of female autonomy, coupled with the rising expectations that grew out of the renewed prosperity of post-Famine life, enabled a dispossessed generation of women to seize control over their own destinies by seeking new lives abroad.

Nevertheless, some have seen pathology in the adjustment of rural Irish women to American city life. These "daughters of Erin" succumbed to madness, drunkenness, and other anti-social or masochistic behaviors. Others see the theme of exile as being the key to understanding the mass exodus of men and women from nineteenth and early twentieth century Ireland. [4] In contrast to these pessimistic evaluations of the nature of Irish emigration, the actual adjustment of most Irish women in urban America indicates a far more positive reality. In fact, the rapid mobility of young Irish women abroad indicates that for the vast majority of women leaving their homeland in the years between 1885 and 1920, emigration was a welcome route out of dependency into independence. Rather than being passive victims of repression, the young women who left their rural Irish homes regained and expanded their economic and social autonomy in urban America. They saw themselves less as exiles than as entrants into a new world of opportunity. They were not dependent "daughters"; instead, they were independent "sisters," living abroad, who provided the means for their siblings to follow in their wake.

The persistence of delayed and restricted marriage among

the Irish overseas has also been seen as proof that female subordination and gender segregation endured among the Irish after their emigration.[5] But the American Irish abandoned the exaggerated patterns of delayed and restricted marriage when economic necessity no longer made such behavior mandatory. In addition, late marriage was not necessarily detrimental to women. The relatively late marital age among Irish-Americans reflected not animosity between the sexes but rather the high degree of economic and social independence among young Irish women abroad. They did not need the protection of a husband since, unlike the women of other immigrant groups who shunned domestic service, they could easily find work among the expanding middle class in the growing cities of the United States. By postponing marriage, young girls in service earned incomes that could be used to liberate siblings from rural drudgery at home. They could also use their wages for hitherto unimaginable luxuries such as fine dresses, entertainment, or even dowries for their eventual marriages.

Domestic service also freed young Irish women from direct participation in the rough and tumble of laissez-faire capitalism in American cities of the time. Although household service was arduous and the hours long, health and safety conditions for workers in middle class homes were better than those facing women in unregulated factories, sweatshops, and tenements. In addition, their intimate exposure to the refinements of the middle-class way of life facilitated mobility among servants and their children. By learning the manners and mores of the middle class during their time in service, Irish mothers were able to speed the assimilation of their American-born children.

The economic and social choices made by young Irish women in the United States eased their transition from one world to another and reduced the psychological dislocation of an otherwise abrupt entrance into an alien environment. In fact, their successful adaptation to individualistic American life can be measured by their representation in the female work force, their children's rapid social and economic mobility, and their participation in public life—which was far greater than that of other female immigrants in the United States. In fact, if Irish social mobility in the United States is measured by the accomplishments of women, Irish-Americans enjoyed a rapid climb from a gloomy world of rural poverty into a new world of urban prosperity.

Emphasizing the maladjustment of some Irish women to American life clearly does not tell the story of the majority of the young women who left Ireland in the late nineteenth and early twentieth centuries. Instead, although certain retrenchments in Irish economic and social life after the Famine were extremely detrimental to Irish women in the short run, in the long run such changes actually fostered the emigration of these women to the more dynamic world of foreign cities. By most accounts, their lives after emigration surpassed those they could have expected at home, either before or after the Famine. Thus, their emigration must be seen not as an exile but rather as an unprecedented opportunity. More so than their mothers or their grandmothers before them or their sisters at home, the young women who left Ireland between 1885 and 1920 were the first generation of Irish women to realize fully their own social and economic modernization as women.

The years of the late nineteenth and early twentieth centuries were troubled ones for Ireland. Prosperity remained elusive, and political turmoil persisted. Under the slogan "Ourselves Alone," the Irish sought independence from Britain, seeing British control as the key to Irish distress. Throughout the period, increasing numbers of men joined the armed struggle to wrest Ireland's destiny from the hands of the British Parliament. "Ourselves Alone" appears, however, to have meant something quite different to many women living in rural Ireland in those years. Rather than entering the campaign to liberate Celtic Ireland from the hated Saxon, something male-dominated Nationalist circles discouraged them from doing in any case, women liberated themselves from a society and an economy that had dispossessed them. While their male contemporaries were creating an independent Ireland, the women who left Ireland between 1885 and 1920 were recreating independence for themselves abroad. James Connally's 1915 dictate that "none [were] so fitted to break the chains as those who wear them" applied as much to the women leaving Ireland as it did to its intended audience, the striking workers of Dublin.[6] These women were indeed capable of breaking the chains that bound them, by themselves, alone.

Appendix

Table A.1. Emigration by Province, Ireland, 1851-1920

Years	Leinster	Munster	Ulster	Connaught	Total
1851-1860	233,331	430,409	336,265	136,111	1,136,116
1861-1870	149,794	306,063	201,984	114,059	771,900
1871-1880	111,046	180,868	240,299	86,290	618,503
1881-1890	138,662	251,539	218,645	161,860	770,706
1891-1900	50,376	178,010	87,021	118,119	433,526
1901-1910	42,490	112,350	105,980	85,133	345,953
1911-1920	23,642	37,014	59,961	34,248	154,865
TOTAL	749,341	1,496,253	1,250,155	735,820	4,231,569

Sources: Census for Ireland and the Emigration Returns of the Registrar General of Ireland, 1851-1920, in *Irish Historical Statistics,* ed. W. E. Vaughn and A. J. Fitzpatrick (Dublin: Royal Irish Academy, 1978), table 58, pp. 344-53. Totals calculated by the author.

Table A.2. Population by Province, Ireland, 1881-1926

Year	Leinster	Munster	Ulster	Connaught	Total
1881	1,278,989	1,331,115	1,743,075	821,657	5,174,836
1891	1,187,760	1,172,402	1,619,814	724,774	4,704,750
1901	1,152,829	1,076,188	1,582,826	646,932	4,458,775
1911	1,162,044	1,035,495	1,581,696	610,984	4,390,219
1926	1,149,092	969,902	1,556,652[a]	552,907	4,228,553
LOSS	−129,987	−361,213	−186,423	−268,750	−946,283

Source: Census for Ireland, in *Irish Historical Statistics,* ed. W.E. Vaughan and A.J. Fitzpatrick (Dublin: Royal Irish Academy, 1978), tables 6 and 7, pp. 15, 16, 24. Totals calculated by the author. The population increase of 9,215 recorded in Leinster between 1901 and 1911 reflects the growth of Dublin in those years and does not indicate any trend toward population increase in rural areas.

[a] Estimated total for Northern Ireland and the three counties.

Table A.3. Emigration by Sex, Ireland, 1885-1920

Years	Males	Females	Total
1885-1890	214,896	203,670	418,566
1891-1900	201,570	231,956	433,526
1901-1910	172,297	173,656	345,953
1911-1920	75,879	74,877	150,756
TOTAL	664,642	684,159	1,348,801

Sources: Emigration Statistics of Ireland, 1885-1920, and the Census for Ireland in *Irish Historical Statistics,* ed. W.E. Vaughan and A.J. Fitzpatrick (Dublin: Royal Irish Academy, 1978), table 54, pp. 262, 263. Totals calculated by the author.

Table A.4. Marital Status, All Age Groups, Ireland, 1881-1926

	Males			Females		
Year	Single	Married or Widowed	Total	Single	Married or Widowed	Total
1881	1,740,360	792,402	2,532,762	1,675,737	965,616	2,641,353
1891	1,613,804	705,149	2,318,953	1,527,762	858,035	2,385,797
1901	1,533,515	666,525	2,200,040	1,456,797	801,938	2,258,735
1911	1,510,664	681,384	2,192,048	1,392,150	806,021	2,198,171
1926[a]	1,040,302	466,587	1,506,889	913,796	551,307	1,465,103

Source: Census for Ireland, 1881-1926, in *Irish Historical Statistics,* ed. W.E. Vaughan and A.J. Fitzpatrick (Dublin: Royal Irish Academy, 1978), tables 27 and 28, pp. 88-91.

[a] Free State.

Table A.5. Marital Status, Population Aged Fifteen to Forty-Four, Ireland, 1881-1926

	Males			Females		
Year	Single	Married or Widowed	Total	Single	Married or Widowed	Total
1881	737,875	327,051	1,064,926	691,934	472,131	1,164,065
1891	745,192	268,234	1,013,426	676,882	390,272	1,067,154
1901	744,979	262,007	1,006,986	681,183	368,230	1,049,413
1911	728,805	262,755	991,560	623,043	357,423	980,466
1926[a]	486,331	118,511	604,842	395,393	231,458	626,851

Source: Census for Ireland, 1881-1926, in *Irish Historical Statistics,* ed. W.E. Vaughan and A.J. Fitzpatrick (Dublin: Royal Irish Academy, 1978), tables 27 and 28, pp. 88-91.
[a] Free State.

Table A.6. Population Aged Fifteen to Forty-Four as Percentage of the Total Population, Ireland, 1881-1926

				% of Total Population	
Year	Males	Females	Total	Males	Females
1881	1,064,926	1,164,065	5,174,836	21	22
1891	1,013,426	1,067,154	4,704,750	22	23
1901	1,006,986	1,049,413	4,458,775	23	24
1911	991,560	980,466	4,390,219	23	22
1926[a]	604,842	626,851	2,971,992	20	21

Source: Census for Ireland, 1881-1926, in *Irish Historical Statistics,* ed. W.E. Vaughan and A.J. Fitzpatrick (Dublin: Royal Irish Academy, 1978), tables 27 and 28, pp. 88-91.
[a] Free State.

Notes

Introduction: Going Alone

1. Between 1885 and 1920, 1,357,831 emigrants left Ireland, 684,159 of whom were female. Of these females, an average of 89 percent were single at the time of their departure, and most were under the age of twenty-four. The numerical data cited in this study derive from raw census and emigration figures in the following sources, except where otherwise noted: *Emigration Statistics of Ireland* (Dublin: Alexander Thom, yearly); *Irish Historical Statistics: Population, 1821-1971,* ed. W.E. Vaughan and A.J. Fitzpatrick (Dublin: Royal Irish Academy, 1978); and *International Migrations,* ed. Walter F. Willcox and Imre Ferenczi, 2 vols., National Bureau of Economic Research (New York: Gordon and Breach, 1969). All conclusions based on these data are my own.

2. Brinley Thomas, *Migration and Economic Growth: A Study of Great Britain and the Atlantic Economy* (Cambridge: Cambridge Univ. Press, 1954), p. 78.

3. Oscar Handlin, *The Uprooted: The Epic Story of the Great Migrations That Made the American People* (New York: Grosset and Dunlap, 1951).

4. Rudolph J. Vecoli, " 'Contadini' in Chicago: A Critique of *The Uprooted,*" *Journal of American History* 51:3 (Dec. 1964): 404-17; Virginia Yans-McLaughlin, *Family and Community: Italian Immigrants in Buffalo, 1880-1930* (Ithaca, N. Y.: Cornell Univ. Press, 1977); Virginia Yans-McLaughlin, "A Flexible Tradition: South Italian Immigrants Confront a New York Experience," *Journal of Social History* 7:4 (Summer 1974): 429-45; Virginia Yans-McLaughlin, "Patterns of Work and Family Organization: Buffalo's Italians," *Journal of Interdisciplinary History* 2:2 (Autumn 1971): 299-314.

5. The following is a representative list of other studies that, like Vecoli's and Yans-McLaughlin's, emphasize the male-dominated family composition of European female emigration in the late nineteenth and early twentieth centuries: Thomas Kessner, *The Golden Door: Italian and Jewish Immigrant Mobility in New York City, 1880-1915* (New York: Oxford University Press, 1977); Corinne Azen Krause, "Urbanization without

Breakdown: Italian, Jewish, and Slavic Immigrant Women in Pittsburgh, 1900-1945," *Journal of Urban History* 4:3 (May 1978): 291-306; Charlotte Baum, Paula Hyman, and Sonya Michel, *The Jewish Woman in America* (New York: Dial, 1976); Humbert S. Nelli, "Ethnic Group Assimilation: The Italian Experience," in *Cities in American History,* ed. Kenneth T. Jackson and Stanley K. Schultz (New York: Knopf, 1972), pp. 199-215; Moses Rischen, *The Promised City: New York's Jews, 1870-1914* (New York: Harper Torchbooks, 1962); Jean Scarpaci, ed., "Immigrant Women and the City—Introduction," *Journal of Urban History* 4:3 (May 1978): 251-53; Maxine S. Seller, "Beyond the Stereotype: A New Look at the Immigrant Woman, 1880-1924," *Journal of Ethnic Studies* 3:1 (Spring 1975): 59-70; Maxine S. Seller, "The Education of the Immigrant Woman: 1900-1935," *Journal of Urban History* 4:3 (May 1975): 307-30; Rudolf Glanz, *The Jewish Woman in America: Two Female Immigrant Generations, 1820-1929,* vol. 1, *The Eastern European Jewish Woman;* and vol. 2, *The German Jewish Woman* (KTAV Publishing House and the National Council of Jewish Women, 1976). A recent exception to this rule is Doris Weatherford, *Foreign and Female: Immigrant Women in America, 1840-1930* (New York: Schocken Books, 1986).

6. See the following for a discussion of the impact of social change on women's lives: Patricia Branca and Peter N. Stearns, "Modernization of Women in the Nineteenth Century," *The Forum Series* (St. Louis, Mo.: Forum Press, 1973); Joan Scott and Louise Tilly, "Women's Work and the Family in Nineteenth Century Europe," *Comparative Studies in Society and History* 17:1 (Jan. 1975): 36-64; Edward Shorter, "Female Emancipation, Birth Control and Fertility in European History," *American Historical Review* 78:3 (June 1973): 605-40; Evelyne Sullerot, *Woman, Society and Change,* trans. Margaret Scotford Archer (New York: McGraw-Hill, 1971); Louise A. Tilly and Joan W. Scott, *Women, Work, and the Family* (New York: Holt, Rinehart and Winston, 1978); Louise A. Tilly, Joan W. Scott, and Miriam Cohen, "Women's Work and European Fertility Patterns," *Journal of Interdisciplinary History* 6:3 (Winter 1976): 447-76.

7. For further discussion of the state of Irish archives, see Herbert Wood, "The Public Records of Ireland Before and After 1922," *Transactions of the Royal Irish Historical Society* (4th Series) 13 (1930): 17-49; Margaret Griffith, "A Short Guide to the Public Record Office of Ireland," *Irish Historical Studies* 8:29 (March 1952): 45-58; L.M. Cullen, "Private Sources for Economic and Social History," *Irish Archives Bulletin* 2:1 (1972): 5-25; and Stephen A. Royle, "Irish Manuscript Census Records: A Neglected Source of Information," *Irish Geography* 11: (1978): 110-25.

8. For an overview of the reliability of early Irish censuses, see L.A. Clarkson, "Irish Population Revisited, 1687-1821," in *Irish Population, Economy, and Society: Essays in Honour of the Late K.H. Connell,* ed. J.M. Goldstrom and L.A. Clarkson (Oxford: Clarendon Press, 1981), pp. 13-36.

9. William Macafee, "Local Historical Studies of Rural Areas: Methods and Sources," *Irish Archives Bulletin* 3:6 (1976): 1-31; Vaughan and Fitzpatrick, *Irish Historical Statistics,* "Introduction," pp. xi-xvii.

10. For example, see Joel Mokyr, *Why Ireland Starved: A Quantitative and Analytical History of the Irish Economy, 1800-1850* (London: Allen and Unwin, 1983).

11. Arnold Schrier, *Ireland and the American Emigration, 1850-1900,* 2d ed. (New York: Russell and Russell, 1970).

12. Kerby A. Miller, *Emigrants and Exiles: Ireland and the Irish Exodus to North America* (New York: Oxford Univ. Press, 1985).

13. Ruth-Ann Harris, *The Search for Missing Friends: Irish Immigrant Advertisements Placed in the Boston "Pilot,"* vol. 1, *1831-1850* (Boston: New England Historical Genealogical Society, forthcoming).

14. David Fitzpatrick, *Irish Emigration, 1801-1921* (Dublin: Dundalgan Press, 1984), p. 47.

15. Helga E. Jacobson, "Doing Ethnography: Irish Community Studies and the Exclusion of Women," *Atlantis* 8:1 (Fall 1982): 1-12.

16. For instance, Kevin O'Neill's *Family and Farm in Pre-Famine Ireland: The Parish of Killashandra* (Madison: Univ. of Wisconsin Press, 1984) offers an excellent analysis of the importance of textile production and butter making in a pre-Famine community, but it does not discuss the role of women in these economic ventures.

17. Conrad M. Arensberg and Solon T. Kimball, *Family and Community in Ireland* (Cambridge: Harvard Univ. Press, 1940). See also Hugh Brody, *Inishkillane: Change and Decline in the West of Ireland* (New York: Schocken Books, 1974); Walter Goldschmidt and Evalyn J. Kunkel, "The Structure of the Peasant Family," *American Anthropologist* 73:5 (Oct. 1971): 1058-76; Alexander J. Humphreys, *New Dubliners: Urbanization and the Irish Family* (London: Routledge and Kegan Paul, 1966); John C. Messenger, *Inis Beag: Isle of Ireland* (New York: Holt, Rinehart and Winston, 1969).

18. Hasia Diner, *Erin's Daughters in America: Irish Immigrant Women in the Nineteenth Century* (Baltimore: Johns Hopkins Univ. Press, 1983).

19. Pauline Jackson, "Women in Nineteenth Century Irish Emigration," *International Migration Review* 18:4 (Winter 1984): 1004-20.

20. Lynn Hollen Lees, *Exiles of Erin: Irish Migrants in Victorian London* (Ithaca, N. Y.: Cornell Univ. Press, 1979).

21. Robert E. Kennedy, *The Irish: Emigration, Marriage and Fertility* (Berkeley: Univ. of California Press, 1973).

22. Margaret MacCurtain and Donncha O'Corrain, eds., *Women in Irish Society: The Historical Dimension* (Westport, Conn.: Greenwood Press, 1979).

23. See the archives of the WPA Writers' Project: A Study of Connecticut's Ethnic Groups in the 1930s, boxes 1-93, University of Connecticut, Storrs, Conn.; and the Peoples of Connecticut Oral History Project, Irish interviews 1-26, May 1975, Center for Oral History, University of Connecticut, Storrs, Conn., for some examples.

24. As Alan M. Kraut's *Huddled Masses: The Immigrant in American Society, 1880-1921* (Arlington Heights, Ill.: Harlan Davidson, 1982) has shown, immigration was an active choice made by individuals.

1. The Changing Face of Ireland, 1830-1880

1. There has been some debate over the benefits of the potato diet on the health of the Irish, however. For instance, the *Dublin University Magazine* of December 1836 reported that the populations of Leitrim, Sligo, and Mayo, regions heavily dependent on subsistence potato cultivation, "have been . . . exposed to the worst effects of hunger and ignorance. . . . The consequences of two centuries of degradation and hardship exhibit themselves in the whole physical condition of the people. . . . [They are f]ive feet two upon an average, pot-bellied [perhaps from severe malnutrition], bow-legged, abortively featured." Other observers were not convinced that the potato diet of the Irish caused them physical harm. For instance, Arthur Young, writing about Kerry, Cork, and Limerick in 1780, noted, "The food of the common Irish is potatoes and milk; it is said not to be sufficiently nourishing for the support of hard labour . . . [yet] many of these poor people are as athletic in their form, as robust, and as capable of enduring labour as any upon earth." See F. Edmund Hogan, S.J., *The Irish People: Their Height, Form, and Strength,* (Dublin: M.H. Gill and Son, 1899), pp. 26, 27, 64.

2. Mokyr, *Why Ireland Starved,* p. 9.

3. Hutton, "Statistical Survey of the County of Clare," 1808, p. 168, cited in Hogan, *The Irish People,* pp. 73-74.

4. C.H. Oldham, "The Incidence of Emigration on Town and Country Life in Ireland," *Journal of the Statistical and Social Inquiry Society of Ireland* 13:94 (Nov.-June 1914): 207.

5. For a discussion of Ireland's peripheral position in British economic development, see Michael Hechter, *Internal Colonialism: The Celtic Fringe in British National Development, 1536-1966* (Berkeley: Univ. of California Press, 1975). Mokyr's *Why Ireland Starved* and O'Neill's *Family and Farm* are two important updates on the key issue of Ireland's lack of agricultural and industrial development despite high population growth rates in the first half of the nineteenth century.

6. K.H. Connell, "Marriage in Ireland After the Famine: The Diffusion of the Match," *Journal of the Statistical and Social Inquiry Society of Ireland* 19:109 (1955-1956): 96.

7. T.J. Rawson, *The Statistical Survey of the County of Kildare* (1807), p. 23, cited in K. H. Connell, *The Population of Ireland, 1750-1845* (Westport, Conn.: Greenwood Press, 1975), p. 51.

8. Varying estimates of the changing average age at marriage over time can be found in Lees, *Exiles,* p. 147; James S. Donnelly, Jr., *The Land and the People of Nineteenth Century Cork: The Rural Economy and the Land Question* (London: Routledge and Kegan Paul, 1975), p. 221; Gearoid O'Tuathaigh, "The Role of Women in Ireland under the New English Order," in *Women in Irish Society,* p. 3.

9. This statistic was compiled from estimates of the marriage rate found in Lees, *Exiles,* pp. 147, 143; Arensberg and Kimball, *Family,* p. 150; Barbara L. Solow, *The Land Question and the Irish Economy, 1870-1903,*

Harvard Economic Studies, vol. 139 (Cambridge: Harvard Univ. Press, 1971), p. 101; James Meenan, "Some Causes and Consequences of the Low Irish Marriage Rate," *Journal of the Statistical and Social Inquiry Society of Ireland* 15 (1932-1933): 20; Brendan Walsh, "Marriage Rates and Population Pressure: Ireland, 1871 and 1911," *Economic History Review* (2d series) 23:1 (April 1970): 148; "Reports of the Registrar General for Ireland, 1864-1920," in *Historical Statistics*, table 44, p. 246.

10. Domhnall MacCarthaigh, "Marriage and Birth Rates for Knockainy Parish, 1882-1941," *Journal of the Cork Historical and Archaeological Society* (2d series, pt. 1) 47:165 (Jan.-June 1942): 5.

11. Mokyr, *Why Ireland Starved*, p. 33.

12. These numbers are based on estimates of household size found in Meenan, "Some Causes and Consequences," p. 19; Lees, *Exiles*, pp. 125, 127; O'Neill, *Family and Farm*, pp. 167-69; L.A. Clarkson, "Irish Population Revisited, 1687-1821," in *Irish Population, Economy, and Society: Essays in Honour of the Late K.H. Connell*, ed. J.M. Goldstrom and L.A. Clarkson (New York: Oxford Univ. Press, 1981), p. 32; Joseph Lee, "On the Accuracy of Pre-Famine Censuses," in Goldstrom and Clarkson, *Irish Population*, p. 53.

13. Reports of the Registrar General for Ireland, 1864-1920, in *Historical Statistics*, table 43, p. 244.

14. MacCarthaigh, "Knockainy," p. 5; Brody, *Inishkillane*, p. 75; Brendan Walsh, *Some Irish Population Problems Reconsidered* (Dublin: Economic and Social Research Institute, paper no. 42, 1968), p. 6.

15. Grant, *Impressions of Ireland*, cited in Hogan, *The Irish People*, p. 83.

16. Several sources corroborate the existence of relative prosperity in late eighteenth- and very early nineteenth-century Ireland and the reasons for its demise after 1830. Among them are Mokyr, *Why Ireland Starved;* Samuel Clark, *Social Origins of the Irish Land War* (Princeton: Princeton Univ. Press, 1979); John E. Pomfret, *The Struggle for Land in Ireland, 1800-1923* (Princeton: Princeton Univ. Press, 1930); Woodham-Smith, *The Great Hunger: Ireland, 1845-1849*; Ruth-Ann Harris, "Internal and External Migration as Alternatives: The Case of the Pre-Famine Irish" (Boston, 1981, Mimeographed); S.H. Cousens, "The Regional Pattern of Emigration during the Great Irish Famine, 1846-1851," *Transactions and Papers of the Institute of British Geographers* no. 28 (1960): 125.

17. S.H. Cousens, "The Regional Death Rates in Ireland during the Great Famine from 1846 to 1851," *Population Studies* 14:1 (July 1960): 55.

18. Connell, *Population*, p. 90.

19. T. Campbell, *A Philosophical Survey of the South of Ireland* (1777), p. 147, cited in Connell, *Population*, p. 51.

20. These numbers were found in Connell, *Population*, p. 90; Clark, *Land War*, p. 53; Woodham-Smith, *Hunger*, p. 34; L.M. Cullen, *An Economic History of Ireland Since 1660* (New York: Barnes and Noble, 1972), p. 136; J.N.H. Douglas, "Emigration and Irish Peasant Life," *Ulster Folklife* 9 (1963): 11.

21. Pomfret, *Struggle*, p. 17.

22. Population densities can be found in W.F. Adams, *Ireland and the Irish Emigration to the New World from 1815 to the Famine* (New Haven: Yale Univ. Press, 1932), p. 5.

23. Clark, *Land War,* p. 24; Pomfret, *Struggle,* pp. 3, 11, 20, 22, 23.

24. O'Neill, *Family and Farm,* pp.102-7.

25. Samuel Clark and James S. Donnelly, Jr., "Introduction, Part I: The Tradition of Violence and Political Unrest, 1780-1914," in *Irish Peasants: Violence and Political Unrest, 1780-1914,* ed. Samuel Clark and James S. Donnelly, Jr. (Madison: Univ. of Wisconsin Press, 1983), p. 31.

26. Pomfret, *Struggle,* p. 28.

27. Freeman, *Ireland,* pp. 119, 129; Cullen, *Economic History,* p. 137.

28. Cormac O'Grada, "Seasonal Migration and Post-Famine Adjustment in the West of Ireland," *Studia Hibernica* 13 (1973): 52, 65, 75 and Harris, p. 15.

29. Joel Mokyr, "Industrialization and Poverty in Ireland and the Netherlands," *Journal of Interdisciplinary History* 10:3 (Winter 1980): 434, 429; Douglas, "Emigration," p. 11.

30. Canon P.A. Shehan, *The Blindness of Dr. Gray* (Dublin: Phoenix, 1909), p. 224, cited in K.H. Connell, "The Land Legislation and Irish Social Life," *Economic History Review* (2d series) 11:1(1958): 3.

31. Goldschmidt and Kunkel, "Peasant Family," p. 1065; Cormac O'Grada, "Primogeniture and Ultimogeniture in Rural Ireland," *Journal of Interdisciplinary History* 10:3 (Winter 1980): 491.

32. Quoted in Arensberg and Kimball, *Family,* pp. 202, 366; K.H. Connell, "Peasant Marriage in Ireland: Its Structure and Development Since the Famine," *Economic History Review* (2d series) 14:3 (April 1962): 503-5.

33. Quoted in Donnelly, *Cork,* p. 224.

34. Quoted in Brody, *Inishkillane,* p. 112.

35. Clark, *Land War,* p. 107.

36. Freeman, *Ireland,* p. 183.

37. These numbers were derived from data in Schrier, *Emigration,* p. 80; Clark, *Land War,* p. 141; Cullen, *Economic History,* p. 138.

38. In fact, the diversification of the Irish diet after the Famine may actually have decreased the nutrition available to the rural population. As store-bought tea, sugar, and Indian meal became more common, the intake of potatoes fell. As a result, the Irish succumbed to a "junk food" frenzy at the expense of the far more nourishing potato and milk diet common earlier in the century. One study of the deteriorating nutritional value of the post-Famine diet points to the increasing incidence of pellagra—a nutritional deficiency disease—caused by substituting corn or "Indian" meal for the more vitamin- and mineral-laden potatoes. See E. Margaret Crawford, "Indian Meal and Pellagra in Nineteenth Century Ireland," in Goldstrom and Clarkson, *Population,* pp. 113-34.

39. John Archer Jackson, *The Irish in Britain* (London: Routledge and Kegan Paul, 1963), p. 101.

40. Cullen, *Economic History,* p. 140; L.M. Cullen, *Life in Ireland* (New York: Putnam, 1968), p. 144.

41. Cullen, *Economic History*, pp.144, 146, 147.

42. For a full discussion of the condition of Irish manufacturing and industry after the Famine, see A.C. Hepburn, "Catholics in the North of Ireland, 1850-1921: The Urbanization of a Minority," in *Minorities in History*, ed. A.C. Hepburn (London: Edward Arnold, 1978); L.M. Cullen, *Life; Economic History;* and *Six Generations: Life and Work in Ireland from 1790* (Cork: Mercier, 1970); Humphreys, *Dubliners;* Freeman, *Ireland;* Schrier, *Emigration;* Clark, *Land War.*

43. Irish interview no. 22, Peoples of Connecticut, May 1975.

44. Irish interview no. 3, ibid.

45. Irish interview no. 9, ibid.

46. Mokyr, *Why Ireland Starved*, p. 230.

47. Mageean, "Migrant Families," pp. 4, 5.

48. Since official emigration statistics for Ireland do not exist until 1851, halfway through the Famine decade, estimates differ on the exact number of people leaving the country between 1845 and 1850. A sample of these varying estimates can be found in the following: Freeman, *Ireland;* Colin McEvedy and Richard Jones, *Atlas of World Population History* (New York: Facts on File, 1978); Willcox and Ferenczi, *International Migrations;* Oliver MacDonagh, "Irish Emigration to the United States of America and the British Colonies During the Famine," in *The Great Famine: Studies in Irish History, 1845-1852,* ed. Robert Dudley Edwards and T. Desmond Williams (New York: New York Univ. Press, 1857).

49. Between 1841 and 1851, Connaught's population fell by 29 percent and Munster's by 22 percent, mostly because of Famine mortality. In those same years, Leinster's population decreased by 15 percent and Ulster's by 16 percent, mostly because of emigration. See the censuses for Ireland, 1841 and 1851, in *Historical Statistics,* table 6, pp. 15-16.

50. Emigration Returns for the Registrar General of Ireland, 1851-1880, in *Historical Statistics,* table 34, pp. 261-62.

51. In the 1850s, while the east lost 13 percent and the south almost 19 percent of their populations, the west lost less than 10 percent of its people. Only Ulster demonstated a slower rate of population loss in the 1850s: during that decade the north's population fell by only 5 percent. By the 1870s, however, Ulster's population loss of 5 percent matched that of Ireland as a whole, while Connaught's population loss of only 3 percent during that decade was well below the countrywide average. In fact, in 1876 and 1877 Ireland's population increased by 8,836 people, and most of this population growth took place in the west and the southwest. See the censuses for Ireland for the years in question in *Historical Statistics,* table 6, pp. 15-16.

52. Cormac O'Grada, "Post-Famine Adjustment: Essays in Nineteenth Century Irish Economic History," *Irish Social and Economic History* 1 (1974): 65.

53. See the appendix for emigration numbers by province between 1851 and 1880.

2. Women and Social Change, 1830-1880

1. Census for Ireland, 1841, cited in Clark, *Land War,* p. 50; Connell, "Land Legislation," p. 2.

2. Lees, *Exiles,* pp. 141-45; Damian Hannan, *Displacement and Development: Class, Kinship and Social Change in Irish Rural Communities* (Dublin: 1979), pp. 43-46.

3. Bertram Hutchinson. "On the Study of Non-Economic Factors in Irish Economic Development," *Economic and Social Review* 1:4 (July 1970): 523.

4. WPA, box 17, file 109.2, "The Irish in Bridgeport," interview with William N., 1939.

5. For instance, see Brody, *Inishkillane;* K.H. Connell, *Irish Peasant Society: Four Historical Essays* (Oxford: Clarendon Press, 1968); Connell, *Population;* Connell, "Land Legislation;" Donnelly, *Cork;* Lees, *Exiles;* O'Tuathaigh, "Women"; Joseph J. Lee, "Woman and the Church Since the Famine," in MacCurtain and O'Corrain, *Women in Irish Society;* Adams, *Emigration.*

6. Connell, *Society,* pp. 52-58

7. Connell, *Society,* pp. 82, 53-57, 62-65; Harris, "Migration," p. 15.

8. Connell, *Society,* p. 82.

9. For the status of the Church before the Famine, see Larkin, "Economic Growth" and "Devotional Revolution"; S.J. Connolly, *Priests and People in Pre-Famine Ireland, 1780-1845* (New York: St. Martin's Press, 1982); and Patrick Corish, *The Irish-Catholic Experience: A Historical Survey* (Dublin: Gill and MacMillan, 1985). See also Thomas G. Conway, "Women's Work in Ireland," *Eire-Ireland* 7:1 (1972): 16; Adams, *Emigration,* p. 64; Lees, *Exiles,* p. 179; Clark, *Land War,* p. 59.

10. Several accounts of pre-Famine Irish life have remarked on the relative equality of wives and husbands within the family. See Brody, *Inishkillane;* Lees, *Exiles;* Sheridan Gilley, "English Attitudes towards the Irish," in *Immigrants and Minorities in British Society,* ed. Colin Holmes (London: Allen and Unwin, 1978), pp. 81-110; Hannan, *Displacement;* Joseph Lee, "Marriage and Population in Pre-Famine Ireland," *Economic History Review* (2d series) 21:2 (Aug. 1968): 283-95.

11. Humphreys, *Dubliners,* p. 18; Lynn Hollen Lees and John Modell, "The Irish Countryman Urbanized: A Comparative Perspective on the Famine Migration," *Journal of Urban History* 3:4 (Aug. 1977): 392; Connell, *Population,* p. 51; Brody, *Inishkillane,* p. 113; Douglas, "Emigration," p. 11; Hutchinson, "Non-Economic Factors," p. 524.

12. Connell, *Population,* pp. 125, 15, 49, 127, 128; Estyn Evans, "Peasant Beliefs in Nineteenth Century Ireland," in *Views of the Irish Peasantry, 1800-1916,* ed. Daniel J. Casey and Robert E. Rhodes (Hamden, Conn.: Archon Books, 1977), p. 42; G.L.S. Tucker, "Irish Fertility Rates Before the Famine," *Economic History Review* (2d series) 23:2 (Aug. 1970): 278.

13. Timothy O'Neill, *Life and Tradition in Rural Ireland* (London: J.M. Dent and Sons, 1977), p. 61.

14. Lee, "Women and the Church," p. 37.

15. Cullen, *Generations,* p. 26; Mary E. Daly, "Women, Work and Trade Unionism," in MacCurtain and O'Corrain, *Women in Irish Society,* p. 71; Lee, "Women and the Church," p. 37; Humphreys, *Dubliners,* p. 13; Douglas, "Emigration," p. 11; Hasia Diner, "Immigrant Women, Voluntary Associations, and the Process of Adaptation to Urban America" (Cambridge, Mass., 1980, Mimeographed), pp. 6, 7; Margaret MacCurtain, "Women, the Vote and Revolution," in MacCurtain and O'Corrain, *Women in Irish Society,* p. 46; L.M. Cullen, "Problems in the Interpretation and Revision of Eighteenth Century Irish Economic History," *Transactions of the Royal Irish Historical Society* (5th series) 17 (1967): 20; Woodham-Smith, *Hunger,* p. 33; Hannan, *Displacement,* p. 47; Harris, "Migration," p. 8; Lees, *Exiles,* p. 147; Census for Ireland, 1841, "Condition of the Poorer Classes in Ireland," cited in Lynn Hollen Lees, "Mid-Victorian Migration and the Irish Family Economy," *Victorian Studies* (Autumn 1976): 27-28.

16. Traditional, *Songs, Jigs, Reels, and Ballads of Ireland,* Murray Hill Records, 920344.

17. Arthur Young, *A Tour of Ireland* . . . (London: 1780), cited in Lees, "Mid-Victorian Migration," p. 28.

18. Lee, "Women and the Church," p. 37; Daly, "Women and Trade Unionism," p. 71; Cousens, "Emigration, 1846-1851," p. 125; Connell, *Society,* pp. 56, 26; Cullen, *Generations,* pp. 51, 30, 52-57; Larkin, "Economic Growth," p. 853; Harris, "Migration," p. 6; Macafee, "Methods," p. 17; Cullen, "Problems," p. 20; Griffith, *Population,* p. 62; Evans, "Beliefs," p. 40; Martin J. Waters, "Peasants and Emigrants: Considerations of the Gaelic League as a Social Movement," in Casey and Rhodes, *Irish Peasantry,* p. 160; Adams, *Emigration,* p. 6; Freeman, *Ireland,* p. 202.

19. Cullen, *Generations,* pp. 22; Cullen, *Economic History,* p. 138; Hutchinson, "Non-Economic Factors," p. 516; Adams, *Emigration,* p. 109; Evans, "Beliefs," p. 51.

20. Cullen, *Generations,* pp. 20, 22; Caoimhin O'Danachair, "The Dress of the Irish," *Eire-Ireland* 2:3 (Autumn 1967): 8, 9.

21. Quoted in Cullen, *Generations,* p. 22.

22. Diner, "Immigrant Women," pp. 3, 4; Arensberg and Kimball, *Family,* p. 200; Donnelly, *Cork,* p. 22; Evalyn Michaelson and Walter Goldschmidt, "Female Roles and Male Dominance among Peasants," *Southwestern Journal of Anthropology* 27:4 (Winter 1971): 336; Brody, *Inishkillane,* p. 112.

23. Quoted in Connell, "Peasant Marriage," p. 516.

24. Ibid., pp. 505, 511; Brody, *Inishkillane,* p. 110.

25. Humphreys, *Dubliners,* p. 18.

26. Quoted in Humphreys, *Dubliners,* p. 21.

27. Lee, "Women and the Church," p. 38.

28. Arensberg and Kimball, *Family,* pp. 195, 196, 372; Robert F. Bales, "Attitudes toward Drinking in the Irish Culture," in *Society, Culture, and Drinking Patterns,* ed. David J. Pittman and Charles R. Snyder (New York: Wiley, 1962), pp. 168, 171; Diner, "Immigrant Women," p. 4; Damian Hannan

and L. Katsiaouni, *Traditional Families: From Culturally Prescribed to Negotiated Roles in Irish Farm Families* (Dublin: 1977), pp. 18, 169; John C. Messenger, "Sex and Repression in an Irish Folk Community," in *Human Sexual Behavior: Variations in the Ethnographic Spectrum,* ed. Donald S. Marshall and Robert C. Suggs (New York: Basic Books, 1971), p. 8; John C. Messenger, "Types and Causes of Disputes in an Irish Community," *Eire-Ireland* 3:111 (Fall 1968): 35; Humphreys, *Dubliners,* p. 131.

29. Arensberg and Kimball, *Family,* pp. 197, 206, 208, 203; Evans, "Beliefs," p. 146.

30. WPA, box 17, file 109.2, "The Irish in Bridgeport," interview with Patrick McManus, 1939.

31. Connell, *Society,* p. 82.

32. Larkin, "Devotional Revolution," p. 636.

33. Irish interview no. 6, Peoples of Connecticut, May 1975.

34. George Moore, *The Lake* (1905), cited in Connell, *Society,* p. 128.

35. Quoted from a sermon written by Archbishop McCabe and delivered at all Catholic churches in Dublin in 1881. It was also published in the *Freeman's Journal* in the same year. See Emmet Larkin, *The Roman Catholic Church and the Creation of the Modern Irish State, 1878-1886* (Philadelphia: American Philosophical Society, 1975), pp. 96-97.

36. Larkin, "Devotional Revolution," p. 636.

37. David Fitzpatrick, "The Disappearance of the Irish Agricultural Labourer, 1841-1912," *Irish Economic and Social History* 7 (1980): 84; Oldham, "Emigration," p. 208.

38. WPA, box 17, file 109.2, "The Irish in Bridgeport," interview with Patrick McManus, 1939.

39. These figures are compiled from census data in tables 3, 6, and 12 in Kennedy, *The Irish,* pp. 45, 48, 60.

40. Peig Sayers, *Peig: The Autobiography of Peig Sayers of the Great Blasket Island,* trans. Bryan McMahon (Syracuse, N. Y.: Syracuse Univ. Press, 1974), p. 151.

41. Although Ireland had a system of state-sponsored schools beginning in 1831, no such system existed in England until 1870. Free national schools in Scotland appeared only in 1872. See D.H. Akenson, "National Education and the Realities of Irish Life, 1831-1900," *Eire-Ireland* 4:4 (Winter 1969): 42.

42. For complete discussions of the national schools and British educational policy in Ireland, see D.H. Akenson, *The Irish Education Experiment: The National System of Education in the Nineteenth Century* (London: Routledge and Kegan Paul, 1970); J.M. Goldstrom, *The Social Content of Education, 1808-1870: A Study of the Working-Class School Reader in England and Ireland* (Shannon: Irish Univ. Press, 1972); Lewis Perry Curtis, Jr., *Anglo-Saxons and Celts: A Study of Anti-Irish Prejudice in Victorian England,* Studies in British History and Culture, vol. 2 (Bridgeport, Conn.: Conference on British Studies at the University of Bridgeport, 1968).

43. Humphreys, *Dubliners,* p. 44; Robert S. Fortner, "The Culture of

Hope and the Culture of Despair: The Print Media and 19th Century Irish Emigration," *Eire-Ireland* 13:3 (Fall 1978): 44; Akenson, "National Education," p. 43; Akenson, *Irish Education*, p. 319.

44. Adams, *Emigration*, p. 218; Akenson, "National Education," p. 44; Larkin, "Devotional Revolution," p. 651; Clark, *Land War,* p. 48; Donnelly, *Cork*, p. 249; Willcox and Ferenczi, *Migrations*, p. 269; Akenson, *Irish Education*, pp. 376, 378; James H. Johnson, "Marriage and Fertility in 19th Century Londonderry," *Journal of the Statistical and Social Inquiry Society of Ireland* (pt. 1, 111th sess.) 20 (1957-1958): 101; Lees, *Exiles,* p. 171.

45. Akenson, *Irish Education*, pp. 378, 383, 380; Alf MacLochlainn, "Gael and Peasant—A Case of Mistaken Identity?" in Casey and Rhodes, *Irish Peasantry,* p. 25; Lees, *Exiles,* p. 171.

46. Akenson, *Irish Education*, p. 321; Akenson, "National Education," p. 44.

47. These conclusions are drawn from data in the Census for Ireland, 1851-1901, in Akenson, *Irish Education,* p. 376.

48. These conclusions are drawn from data in Akenson, *Irish Education*.

49. Akenson, *Irish Education,* p. 227.

50. Maurice O'Sullivan, *Twenty Years A-Growing,* trans. Moya Llewellyn Davies and George Thompson, with an introductory note by E.M. Forster (New York: Viking Press, 1935), p. 5.

51. Michael MacGowan, *The Hard Road to Klondike,* trans. Valentin Iremonger (London: Routledge and Kegan Paul, 1962), p. 10.

52. Sayers, *Autobiography,* p. 20.

53. Irish interview no. 6, Peoples of Connecticut, May 1975.

54. Irish interview no. 3, ibid.

55. Irish interview no. 12, ibid.

56. These percentages are drawn from data in the Census for Ireland, 1901, in Akenson, *Irish Education,* p. 378.

57. O'Sullivan, *Twenty Years,* p. 5.

58. MacGowan, *Hard Road,* pp. 10,11.

59. Sayers, *Autobiography,* p. 28.

60. Helen Nolan Need to William F. Nolan, 23 Sept. 1986.

61. Irish interview no. 9, Peoples of Connecticut, May 1975.

62. Lees, *Exiles,* p. 34; Freeman, *Ireland,* pp. 231, 110, 240, 241; Cullen, *Economic History,* pp. 142, 143; Macafee, "Methods," p. 19.

63. Cullen, *Generations,* p. 110.

64. Clark, *Land War,* p. 123.

65. AE (George Russell) in *The Irish Homestead,* Jan. 29, 1910, in *Selections from the Contributions to "The Irish Homestead" by G.W. Russell—AE,* vol. 1, ed. Henry Summerfield (Atlantic Highlands, N.J.: Humanities Press, 1978), p. 23.

66. Michael Hogan to Catherine Nolan, 12 March 1851 and 1 March 1852, in Miss T. Kelly, "Letters from America: New Light on Emigration," *Carloviana: The Journal of the Old Carlow Society* 1:1 (Jan. 1947): 25, 26.

67. Lewis Doyle, 23 Jan. 1873, in Kelly, "Letters from America," p. 28.

3. Women and Emigration, 1880-1920

1. WPA, box 17, file 109.2, "The Irish in Bridgeport," interview with Miss K. II, 1939.

2. J. Greaves, 10 June 1837, and E. Toner, 21 Jan. 1819, quoted in Miller, *Emigrants and Exiles,* p. 205.

3. Adams, *Emigration,* p. 137; Daly, *Social and Economic History,* pp. 63-66.

4. J. Curtain, 23 June 1829, quoted in Miller, *Emigrants and Exiles,* p. 207.

5. Mageean, "Migrant Families," p. 7; Terry Coleman, *Going to America* (Garden City, N.Y.: Anchor, 1973), p. 8.

6. A.C. Buchanan, *Emigration Practically Considered 1826-1827,* quoted in Adams, *Emigration,* p. 192.

7. Harris, "Migration," p. 9.

8. Cousens, "Mortality during the Irish Famine," p. 127; Gordon F. Streib, "Old Age in Ireland: Demographic and Sociological Aspects," *Gerontologist* 8:4 (Winter 1968): 229; McEvedy and Jones, *Atlas,* p. 46; Freeman, *Ireland,* p. 120.

9. William Bennett, *Narrative of a Recent Journey in Ireland* (London: 1947), p. 53; and H. Donnan, 2 April 1848, quoted in Miller, *Emigrants and Exiles,* p. 294.

10. Mrs. Nolan, ? Oct. 1850, quoted in Miller, *Emigrants and Exiles,* p. 293.

11. H. Lynch, 21 April 1847, quoted in Miller, *Emigrants and Exiles,* p. 292; and Bennett, *Narrative,* quoted in Miller, *Emigrants and Exiles,* p. 298.

12. Coleman, *Going to America,* p. 8; Fitzpatrick, *Irish Emigration, 1801-1921,* p. 23.

13. J. Fleming, 26 Dec. ?, quoted in Miller, *Emigrants and Exiles,* p. 293.

14. O'Grada, "Seasonal Migration," pp. 52, 65, 75; O'Grada, "Post-Famine Adjustment," p. 65; Harris, "Migration," p. 15; Willcox and Ferenczi, *International Migrations,* p. 730; Harkness, "Irish Emigration," pp. 271-72; David Fitzpatrick, "Irish Emigration in the Later Nineteenth Century," *Irish Historical Studies* 22:86 (Sept. 1980): 126; J.A. Jackson, *Irish,* p. 5; S.H. Cousens, "Emigration and Demographic Change in Ireland, 1851-1861," *Economic History Review* (2d series) 14:2 (1961): 275; Mageean, "Migrant Families," p. 9.

15. Censuses for Ireland and the Emigration Returns for the Registrar General of Ireland, 1881-1920, in *Historical Statistics,* table 58, pp. 344-53. See the appendix for emigration by province between 1851 and 1920.

16. Censuses for Ireland, 1881-1926, in *Historical Statistics,* tables 6 and 7, pp. 15, 16, 24. The population increase of 9,215 recorded in Leinster between 1901 and 1911 reflects the growth of Dublin in those years and does not indicate any trend toward population growth in rural areas of the province. See the appendix for population by province between 1881 and 1926.

17. Irish interview no. 6, Peoples of Connecticut, May 1975.

18. Mageean, "Migrant Families," p. 8; Harris, "Migration," pp. 8, 9; Lees and Modell, "Irish Countryman," p. 401.

19. John Astle, 1826, quoted in Adams, *Emigration,* p. 109.

20. Thompson, "Census, 1911," p. 643; J.A. Jackson, *Irish,* p. 18; Cousens, "Emigration and Demographic Change," p. 275; Thomas, *Migration,* p. 73; Harkness, "Irish Emigration," p. 276; Donnelly, *Cork,* p. 277.

21. W.B. Best, 26 May and 11 Oct. 1862, 15 Aug. 1863, quoted in Miller, *Emigrants and Exiles,* p. 360.

22. Censuses for Ireland, 1885-1920, in *Historical Statistics,* table 58, pp. 344-53. See the appendix for emigration by sex between 1885 and 1920.

23. Julia Lough, 18 Jan. 1891, quoted in Schrier, *Emigration,* p. 38.

24. *Historical Statistics,* table 54, pp. 262-63. Figures for 1909-1911 not available.

25. Sayers, *Autobiography,* p. 129.

26. J. Costello, 20 Nov. 1833, quoted in Miller, *Emigrants and Exiles,* p. 209.

27. Deirdre Mageean, "Nineteenth Century Irish Emigration: A Case Study Using Passenger Lists," in *The Irish in America: Emigration, Assimilation and Impact,* ed. P.J. Drudy (New York: Cambridge Univ. Press, 1985), p. 53.

28. Reports of the Registrar General for Ireland, 1864-1920, in *Historical Statistics,* table 44, p. 246.

29. Censuses for Ireland, 1880-1920, in *Historical Statistics,* tables 27 and 28, pp. 88-91. See the appendix for the marital status of all age groups between 1881 and 1926.

30. These figures were compiled from those in *Historical Statistics.* See the appendix for the marital status of the population aged fifteen to forty-four between 1881 and 1926.

31. These figures are compiled from *Historical Statistics.* See the appendix for the population aged fifteen to forty-four as a percentage of the total population between 1881 and 1926.

32. S.H. Cousens, "Population Trends of Ireland at the Beginning of the Twentieth Century," *Irish Geography* 5 (1964): 396.

33. These conclusions are based on the data in the *Emigration Statistics,* 1885-1916.

34. Harkness, "Irish Emigration," pp. 280-81; Willcox and Ferenczi, *International Migrations,* p. 734.

35. Irish interview no. 9, Peoples of Connecticut, May 1975.

36. Irish interview, no. 3, ibid.

37. Irish interview, no. 18, ibid.

38. WPA, box 17, file 109.2, "The Irish in Bridgeport," interview with Mrs. G., 28 Nov. 1939.

39. Ibid.

4. The Impact of Women's Emigration, 1880-1920

1. These conclusions are based on the population totals for the parish listed in table I, MacCarthaigh, "Knockainy," p. 4.

2. Censuses for Ireland, 1881-1920, in Kennedy, *The Irish,* pp. 58-60.

3. These figures are compiled from the Censuses for Ireland, 1881-1920, in *Historical Statistics,* table 27, pp. 89-90.

4. Larkin, "Economic Growth," p. 854; Meenan, "Marriage," p. 21; Pomfret, *Struggle,* p. 246.

5. Clark, *Land War,* p. 112; Cullen, *Economic History,* pp. 135, 150.

6. Pomfret, *Struggle,* p. 246.

7. Cullen, *Economic History,* p. 149.

8. Ibid.; Schrier, *Emigration,* p. 127.

9. For a full discussion of the land question in the late nineteenth and early twentieth centuries, see Freeman, *Ireland;* Pomfret, *Struggle;* Solow, *Land Question;* Clark, *Land War;* Cullen, *Economic History;* and Erhard Rumpf and A.C. Hepburn, *Nationalism and Socialism in Twentieth Century Ireland* (New York: Barnes and Noble, 1977).

10. John W. Boyle, "A Marginal Figure: The Irish Rural Laborer," in Clark and Donnelly, *Irish Peasants,* p. 331.

11. Larken, "Economic Growth," pp. 852, 853.

12. Freeman, *Ireland,* p. 178; Pomfret, *Struggle,* p. 267; Rumpf and Hepburn, *Nationalism and Socialism,* p. 225.

13. Rumpf and Hepburn, *Nationalism and Socialism,* pp. 225, 226; Freeman, *Ireland,* p. 204.

14. Boyle, "A Marginal Figure," p. 334.

15. WPA, box 17, file 109.2, "The Irish in Bridgeport," interview with anonymous woman no. 2, 1939.

16. Irish interview no. 9, Peoples of Connecticut, May 1975.

17. These percentages are based on numbers in the Census for Ireland, 1911, in *Historical Statistics,* table 25, p. 81, and the Census figures cited in Oldham, "Emigration," p. 210.

18. From "The Agricultural Irish Girl," a traditional nineteenth-century laborers' song. See *Love Poems of the Irish,* ed. Sean Lucy (Cork: Mercier Press, 1967), p. 92.

19. Freeman, *Ireland,* p. 15; D.L. Armstrong, "Social and Economic Conditions in the Belfast Linen Industry, 1850-1900," *Irish Historical Studies,* 7:28 (Sept. 1951: 239; Cullen, *Economic History,* p. 258; Cullen, *Generations,* p. 82; Daly,"Women and Trade Unionism," p. 71; These percentages are based on the figures in the Census for Ireland, 1911, cited in Oldham, "Emigration," p. 210.

20. Oldham, "Emigration," p. 210.

21. Quoted in Emmet Larkin, *James Larkin: Irish Labour Leader, 1876-1947* (Cambridge: MIT Press, 1965), p. 79.

22. Joseph V. O'Brien, *'Dear, Dirty Dublin': A City in Distress, 1899-1916* (Berkeley: Univ. of California Press, 1982), p. 206.

23. Quoted in Larkin, *James Larkin,* p. 134.

24. Cullen, *Economic History,* p. 166; Daly, "Women and Trade Unionism," p. 71.

25. John Finegan, *The Story of Monto: An Account of Dublin's Notorious Red Light District* (Cork: Mercier Mini-Books, 1978), pp. 9, 15.

26. O'Brien, *'Dear, Dirty Dublin,'* pp. 191, 192.

27. Larkin, *James Larkin,* p. 47.

28. Quoted in Larkin, *James Larkin,* p. 134.

29. Finegan, *Monto,* pp. 9, 15.

30. O'Brien, *'Dear, Dirty Dublin,'* p. 117.

31. Ibid., p. 102.

32. Larkin, *James Larkin,* p. 42.

33. O'Brien, *'Dear, Dirty Dublin,'* p. 134.

34. Cullen, *Economic History,* p. 165.

35. Cullen, *Life,* p. 169; Census for Ireland, 1936, in Kennedy, *The Irish,* table 6, p. 48.

36. Freeman, *Ireland,* p. 144.

37. Censuses for Ireland, 1881-1926, 1971, in *Historical Statistics,* table 9, p. 27.

38. *Reports of the Immigration Commission,* table 19, p. 145.

39. Freeman, *Ireland,* p. 119; Lees and Modell, "Irish Countryman," pp. 396, 398; Lees, *Exiles,* p. 32.

40. This percentage is based on the annual numbers in the *Emigration Statistics* and the *Historical Statistics,* table 55, pp. 264, 265.

41. Lees, *Exiles,* p. 44; Harkness, "Irish Emigration," p. 278; Niles Carpenter, *Immigrants and Their Children,* Census Monographs, 1920 (New York: Arno, 1969), p. 169. The female majority among Irish immigrants in urban areas of the United States had existed long before the late nineteenth century, and it continued well into the twentieth century. See also Stephen Steinberg, *Ethnic Myth: Race, Ethnicity, and Class in America* (New York: Atheneum, 1981), and Edward P. Hutchinson, *Immigrants and Their Children, 1850-1950,* Social Science Research Council, U.S. Department of Commerce, Bureau of the Census (New York: Wiley, 1956).

42. These conclusions are based on the *Emigration Statistics,* 1885-1920, and the *Historical Statistics,* table 55, pp. 264, 265.

43. These percentages are from the Census of the United States in the *Reports of the Immigration Commission,* table 95, pp. 805, 806.

44. "The Penalties of Security," trans. Frank O'Connor, in Lucy, *Love Poems,* pp. 83-84.

45. These percentages are based on the numbers in the *Reports of the Immigration Commission,* tables 16-21, pp. 803-20.

46. These percentages are based on the numbers in the Census for Ireland, 1901, pt. 2, *General Report with Illustrative Maps, Diagrams, Tables, and Appendix,* p. 527 [Cd 1190], H.C. 1902, 129, and the *Reports of the Immigration Commission,* tables 12 and 15, pp. 47, 84, and 85.

47. Fortner, "Print Media," p. 46.

48. Anonymous, quoted by Schrier, *Emigration,* p. 115.

49. Irish interview no. 5, Peoples of Connecticut, May 1975.

50. *Emigration Statistics,* 1904-1914; *Reports of the Immigration Commission,* table 39, p. 361.

51. Irish interview no. 6, Peoples of Connecticut, May 1975.

52. In contrast, 18 percent of all Swedish immigrants to the United

States—the only other national group with high levels of unmarried females among its emigrants—returned to their homeland in those same years. U.S. Commissioner-General of Immigration and the Bureau of Immigration and Naturalization in *Reports of the Immigration Commission,* table 37, p. 359; Lars Ljungmark, *Swedish Exodus,* trans. Kermit B. Westerberg (Carbondale, Illinois: Southern Illinois University Press, 1979), p. 141.

5. Irish Women in America, 1880-1920

1. The following comparison of marriage patterns among the Irish in rural Ireland and London is based on the data in the Census for Ireland, 1851 and 1861, and the Census for England, 1851 and 1861, in table A.8, Lees *Exiles,* p. 260.

2. Irish interview no. 17, Peoples of Connecticut, May 1975.

3. WPA, box 17, file 109.2, "The Irish in Bridgeport," interview with Mrs. G., 6 Oct. 1939; interview with anonymous woman no. 2, 1939.

4. Ibid., interview with Mrs. Murphy, 4 Dec. 1939; interview with anonymous woman no. 3, 1939; interview with George, 7 April 1939; interview with anonymous woman no. 2, 1939.

5. Ibid., interview with Mrs. Murphy, 4 Dec. 1939; interview with Mr. D., 26 Oct. 1939.

6. Ibid., interview with Mr. J. Hayes, 20 Nov. 1939; interview with Mrs. T.K., 31 Oct. 1939; interview with Mr. H., 16 Oct. 1939; interview with anonymous woman no. 2, 1939.

7. These figures are compiled from numbers in the Census for Ireland, 1901, in *Historical Statistics,* tables 25 and 43, pp. 80, 245.

8. These figures are compiled from the Census for the United States in table 71, U.S. Congress, Senate, *Reports of the Immigration Commission: Abstracts of Reports of the Immigration Commission with Conclusions and Recommendations and Views of the Minority,* 61st Cong., 3d sess., 1911, S. Doc. 747, p. 429, and table 82, Carpenter, *Immigrants,* p. 18.

9. Irish interview no. 17, Peoples of Connecticut, May 1975.

10. Interview with William F. Nolan, Tiverton, R.I., 10 May 1983.

11. WPA, box 17, file 109.2, "The Irish in Bridgeport," interview with Mrs. G., 6 Oct. 1939; interview with Miss K., 19 Feb. 1940; interview with Mrs. G., 6 Oct. 1939.

12. Ibid., interview with Miss K., 19 Feb. 1940; interview with anonymous woman no. 1, 29 Nov. 1939.

13. Ibid., interview with anonymous woman no. 1, 29 Nov. 1939; interview with William N., 1939; interview with Mrs. G., 6 Oct. 1939.

14. Irish interview no. 4, Peoples of Connecticut, May 1975.

15. WPA, box 17, file 109.2, "The Irish in Bridgeport," interview with Mary Leavy, 4 Oct. 1939.

16. These figures are compiled from the Census for the United States in table 89, *Immigration Commission: Abstracts,* p. 468.

17. These figures are compiled from the Census for the United States in table 88, *Immigration Commission: Abstracts,* p. 464.

18. These figures are compiled from the Census for the United States in table 39, *Immigration Commission, Abstracts,* p. 766.

19. Irish interview no. 13, Peoples of Connecticut, May 1975.

20. Irish interview no. 17, ibid.

21. "Situations Wanted: Females," *New York Times,* June 28, 1873, reproduced in *The Ordeal of Assimilation: A Documentary History of the White Working Class,* ed. Stanley Feldstein and Lawrence Costello (Garden City, N.Y.: Anchor Books, 1974), p. 161.

22. Quoted by Lucy Maynard Salmon, in *Domestic Service* (New York: Macmillan, 1897), p. 147.

23. Quoted in Salmon, *Domestic Service,* p. 210, 154, 155.

24. Quoted in Salmon, *Domestic Service,* p. 126.

25. Rosalyn Baxandall, Linda Gordon, and Susan Reverby, eds., *America's Working Women* (New York: Random House, 1976), pp. 116, 119, 125; James J. Kenneally, *Women and American Trade Unions* (St. Albans, Vt.: Eden Press Women's Publications, 1978), pp. 15, 58, 66, 76; Maurine Weiner Greenwald, *Women, War, and Work: The Impact of World War I on Women Workers in the United States* (Westport, Conn.: Greenwood Press, 1980), p. 206; Gary M. Fink, ed., *Biographical Dictionary of American Labor* (Westport, Conn.: Greenwood Press, 1984), pp. 102, 103, 228, 229, 434, 435, 448, 449, 450, 454, 455.

26. Diner, "Immigrant Women," p. 10.

27. Undated quote in Keena's obituary in the *Journal of the American Irish Historical Society* 20 (1921): 228-30.

28. Fink, *Dictionary,* pp. 277-78.

29. Quoted in John O'Dea, *History of the Ancient Order of Hibernians and the Ladies' Auxiliary,* vol. 3 (Philadelphia: National Board of the AOH, 1923), p. 1123.

30. Interview with William F. Nolan, 10 May 1983. Eventually, Quigley and his neighbors' bonds were redeemed at their full value by the fledgling Free State.

31. Ibid.

32. In contrast, there were eighty-six national organizations for Jewish women alone in that year, according to Diner, "Immigrant Women," p. 2.

33. WPA, box 17, file 109.2, "The Irish in Bridgeport," interview with Mrs. John Hurley, 21 Dec. 1938.

34. Diner, *Daughters,* pp. 125, 137.

35. Irish interview no. 17, Peoples of Connecticut, May 1975.

36. WPA, box 22, file 109.12, "Bridgeport Irish Essays, Oral Histories, Immigration, Organizations, Religion, Occupations, Early Life."

37. WPA, box 45, file 151.2a, "Hartford Ethnic Organizations," L.J. Robertson, Jr., 15 July 1937.

38. An exception to this rule is John O'Grady's *Catholic Charities in the United States: History and Problems* (Washington, D.C.: National Conference of Catholic Charities, 1930).

39. Mary C. Donelin, "American Irish Women 'Firsts,'" *Journal of the American Irish Historical Society* 24 (1925): 215-21.

40. Baxandall, Gordon, and Reverby, *Working Women*, p. 125; Keneally, *Women*, p. 15.

41. WPA, box 17, file 109.2, "The Irish in Bridgeport," interview with Mr. P.S., 16 Nov. 1939.

42. Ibid., interview with Mr. J. Hayes, 20 Nov. 1939; interview with Mr. M. II, 8 Nov. 1939; interview with Mr. D., 26 Oct. 1939; interview with Mr. Ginty, 1939.

43. Ibid., interview with Mr. D., 26 Oct. 1939; interview with Mr. Ginty, 1939.

44. Ibid., interview with Mr. M. II, 8 Nov. 1939.

Conclusion: "Ourselves Alone"

1. Irish interview no. 18, Peoples of Connecticut, May 1975.

2. WPA, box 17, file 109.2, "The Irish in Bridgeport," interview with Mrs. T.K., 31 Oct. 1939.

3. Cornelius McSweeney to John McSweeney, 8 Dec. 1913.

4. For example, see Diner, *Daughters*, and Miller, *Exiles*.

5. Diner, *Daughters*, p. 45.

6. Quoted in the Council for the Status of Women (Ireland), *Irish Women Speak Out—A Plan of Action* (Dublin: Co-op Books, 1981), p. 11.

Selected Bibliography

Very few primary or secondary source materials address the issue of gender in emigration from Ireland in the late nineteenth and early twentieth centuries. As a result, a wide variety of published and unpublished materials dealing with the demographic, economic, and emigration history of Ireland was selected for use in this study. The following selected bibliography includes only those sources actually cited in this work, divided into categories based on subject matter.

Historiography

Clarkson, L.A. "Irish Population Revisited, 1687-1821." In *Irish Population, Economy, and Society: Essays in Honour of the Late K.H. Connell*, edited by J.M. Goldstrom and L.A. Clarkson, pp. 13-26. New York: Oxford Univ. Press, 1981.

Griffith, Margaret. "A Short Guide to the Public Record Office of Ireland." *Irish Historical Studies* 8:29 (March 1952): 45-58.

Jacobson, Helga E. "Doing Ethnography: Irish Community Studies and the Exclusion of Women." *Atlantis* 8:1 (Fall 1982): 1-12.

Lee, J. "On the Accuracy of Pre-Famine Censuses." In *Irish Population, Economy, and Society: Essays in Honour of the Late K.H. Connell*, edited by J.M. Goldstrom and L.A. Clarkson, pp. 37-56. New York: Oxford Univ. Press, 1981.

Macafee, William. "Local Historical Studies of Rural Areas." *Irish Archives Bulletin* 3:6 (1976): 4-31.

Royle, Stephen A. "Irish Manuscript Census Records: A Neglected Source of Information." *Irish Geography* 11 (1978): 110-25.

Wood, Herbert. "The Public Records of Ireland Before and After 1922." *Transactions of the Royal Historical Society* (4th series) 13 (1930): 17-49.

Eyewitness Accounts

Published

Kelly, Miss T. "Letters from America: New Light on Emigration." *Carloviana: The Journal of the Old Carlow Society* 1:1 (Jan. 1947): 25-28.

MacGowan, Michael. *The Hard Road to Klondike.* Translated by Valentin Iremonger. London: Routledge and Kegan Paul, 1962.

O'Sullivan, Maurice. *Twenty Years A-Growing.* Translated by Moya Llewelyn Davies and George Thompson. Introductory note by E.M. Forster. New York: Viking Press, 1935.

Russell, George (AE). *Selections from the Contributions to "The Irish Homestead" by G.W. Russell—A.E.* Edited by Henry Summerfield. Atlantic Highland, N.J.: Humanities Press, 1978.

Sayers, Peig. *Peig: The Autobiography of Peig Sayers of the Great Blasket Island.* Translated by Bryan MacMahon. Syracuse, N.Y.: Syracuse Univ. Press, 1974.

Unpublished

Archives of the WPA Writers' Project: A Study of Connecticut's Ethnic Groups in the 1930s. Boxes 1-93. Univ. of Connecticut, Storrs.

Center for Oral History. The Peoples of Connecticut Oral History Project. Irish Interviews 1-26, May 1975. Univ. of Connecticut, Storrs.

McSweeney, Cornelius. Letter to John McSweeney, 8 Dec. 1913.

Need, Helen Nolan. Letter to William Nolan, 23 Sept. 1986.

Nolan, William. Interview with author. Tiverton, Rhode Island, 10 May 1983.

Numerical Data

Census for Ireland, 1901, pt. #2: *General Report with Illustrative Maps, Diagrams, Tables, and Appendix.* [Cd. 1190]. H.C. 1902.

Emigration Statistics of Ireland, 1885-1908, 1912, 1913-1918, 1920. Dublin: Alexander Thom, 1886-1921.

U.S. Congress. Senate. *Reports of the Immigration Commission: Abstracts of Reports of the Immigration Commission with Conclusions and Recommendations and Views of the Minority.* Vol. 1 of 2. S. Doc. 747. 61st Cong., 3d sess., 1911.

U.S. Congress. Senate. *Reports of the Immigration Commission: Statistical Review of Immigration, 1820-1910; Distribution of Immigrants, 1850-1900.* S. Doc. 756. 61st Cong., 3d sess., 1911.

Vaughan, W.E. and A.J. Fitzpatrick, eds. *Irish Historical Statistics: Population, 1821-1971.* Dublin: Royal Irish Academy, 1978.

Willcox, Walter F., and Imre Ferenczi, eds. *International Migrations*, vol. 1. National Bureau of Economic Research. New York: Gordon and Breach, 1969.

Population

Connell, K.H. "Marriage in Ireland After the Famine: The Diffusion of the Match." *Journal of the Statistical and Social Inquiry Society of Ireland* 19 (1955-56): 82-103.

———. "Peasant Marriage in Ireland: Its Structure and Development Since the Famine." *Economic History Review* (2d series) 14:3 (April 1962): 502-23.

———. *The Population of Ireland, 1750-1845*. Westport, Conn.: Greenwood Press, 1975.

Cousens, S.H. "Regional Death Rates in Ireland during the Great Famine from 1846 to 1851." *Population Studies* 14:4 (July 1960): 55-74.

———. "The Regional Variation in Mortality during the Irish Famine." *Royal Irish Academy Proceedings* 63:3 (Feb. 1963): 127-49.

Griffith, G. Talbot. *Population Problems in the Age of Malthus*. Cambridge: Cambridge Univ. Press, 1926.

Hepburn, A.C. "Catholics in the North of Ireland, 1850-1921: The Urbanization of a Minority." In *Minorities in History*, edited by A.C. Hepburn, pp. 84-101. London: Edward Arnold, 1978.

Johnson, James H. "Marriage and Fertility in 19th Century Londonderry." *Journal of the Statistical and Social Inquiry Society of Ireland* (pt. 1, 111th sess.) 20 (1957-1958): 99-117.

———. "Population Movements in County Derry during a Pre-Famine Year." *Royal Irish Academy Proceedings* (sec. C) 60 (1959): 141-62.

Kennedy, Robert E. *The Irish: Emigration, Marriage and Fertility*. Berkeley: Univ. of California Press, 1973.

Lee, Joseph. "Marriage and Population in Pre-Famine Ireland." *Economic History Review* (2d series) 21:2 (Aug. 1968): 283-95.

MacCarthaigh, Domhnall. "Marriage and Birth Rates for Knockainy Parish, 1882-1941." *Journal of the Cork Historical and Archaeological Society* (series 2, pt. 1) 47:165 (Jan.-June 1942): 4-8.

McEvedy, Colin, and Richard Jones. *Atlas of World Population History*. New York: Facts on File, 1978.

Meenan, James. "Some Causes and Consequences of the Low Irish Marriage Rate." *Journal of the Statistical and Social Inquiry Society of Ireland* (sess. 86) 15 (1932-1933): 19-27.

Streib, Gordon F. "Old Age in Ireland: Demographic and Sociological Aspects." *Gerontologist* 8:4 (Winter 1968): 227-35.

Thomas, Brinley. *Migration and Economic Growth: A Study of Great Britain and the Atlantic Economy.* Cambridge: Cambridge Univ. Press, 1954.

Thompson, Sir William J. "The Census for Ireland, 1911." *Journal of the Royal Statistical Society* (pt. 7) 76 (June 1913): 635-62.

Tucker, G.L.S. "Irish Fertility Rates Before the Famine." *Economic History Review* (2d series) 23:2 (Aug. 1970): 267-84.

Walsh, Brendan M. "Marriage Rates and Population Pressure: Ireland, 1871 and 1911." *Economic History Review* (2d series) 23:1 (April 1970): 148-62.

————. *Some Irish Population Problems Reconsidered.* Dublin: Economic and Social Research Institute, 1968.

Economics

Armstrong, D.L. "Social and Economic Conditions in the Belfast Linen Industry, 1850-1900." *Irish Historical Studies* 7:28 (Sept. 1951): 235-69.

Clark, Samuel. *Social Origins of the Irish Land War.* Princeton: Princeton Univ. Press, 1979.

Connell, K.H. "The Land Legislation and Irish Social Life." *Economic History Review* (2d series) 11:1 (1958): 1-7.

Cullen, L.M. *An Economic History of Ireland Since 1660.* New York: Barnes and Noble, 1972.

————. "Problems in the Interpretation and Revision of Eighteenth Century Irish Economic History." *Transactions of the Royal Historical Society* (5th series) 17 (1967): 1-22.

Daly, Mary E. *Social and Economic History of Ireland Since 1800.* Dublin: Educational Company of Ireland, 1981.

Donnelly, James S., Jr. *The Land and the People of Nineteenth Century Cork: The Rural Economy and the Land Question.* London: Routledge and Kegan Paul, 1975.

Freeman, T.W. *Ireland: A General and Regional Geography.* 4th ed. London: Methuen, 1972.

Hechter, Michael. *Internal Colonialism: The Celtic Fringe in British National Development, 1536-1966.* Berkeley: Univ. of California Press, 1975.

Hutchinson, Bertram. "On the Study of Non-Economic Factors in Irish Economic Development." *Economic and Social Review* 1:4 (July 1970): 509-29.

Larkin, Emmet. "Economic Growth, Capital Investment, and the Roman Catholic Church in Nineteenth Century Ireland." *American Historical Review* 72:3 (April 1967): 852-84.

Mokyr, Joel. "Industrialization and Poverty in Ireland and the Netherlands." *Journal of Interdisciplinary History* 10:3 (Winter 1980): 429-58.

———. *Why Ireland Starved: A Quantitative and Analytical History of the Irish Economy, 1800-1850*. London: Allen and Unwin, 1983.

O'Grada, Cormac. "Post-Famine Adjustment: Essays in Nineteenth Century Irish Economic History." *Irish Economic and Social History* 1 (1974): 65-66.

———. "Primogeniture and Ultimogeniture in Rural Ireland." *Journal of Interdisciplinary History* 10:3 (Winter 1980): 491-97.

O'Neill, Kevin. *Family and Farm in Pre-Famine Ireland: The Parish of Killashandra*. Madison: Univ. of Wisconsin Press, 1984.

Pomfret, John E. *The Struggle for Land in Ireland, 1800-1923*. Princeton: Princeton Univ. Press, 1930.

Rumpf, Erhard, and A.C. Hepburn. *Nationalism and Socialism in Twentieth Century Ireland*. New York: Barnes and Noble, 1977.

Solow, Barbara L. *The Land Question and the Irish Economy, 1870-1903*. Harvard Economic Studies, vol. 139. Cambridge: Harvard Univ. Press, 1971.

Woodham-Smith, Cecil. *The Great Hunger: Ireland, 1845-1849*. New York: Harper and Row, 1962.

Emigration

Adams, W.F. *Ireland and Irish Emigration to the New World from 1815 to the Famine*. New Haven: Yale Univ. Press, 1932.

Coleman, Terry. *Going to Amerca*. Garden City, N.Y.: Anchor Press, 1973.

Cousens, S.H. "Emigration and Demographic Change in Ireland, 1851-1861." *Economic History Review* (2d series) 14:2 (1961): 275-88.

———. "Population Trends in Ireland at the Beginning of the Twentieth Century." *Irish Geography* 5 (1964): 387-401.

———. "The Regional Pattern of Emigration During the Great Irish Famine, 1846-1851." *Transactions and Papers of the Institute of British Geographers* no. 28 (1960): 119-34.

Douglas, J.N.H. "Emigration and Irish Peasant Life." *Ulster Folklife* 9 (1963): 9-19.

Fitzpatrick, David. "The Disappearance of the Irish Agricultural Labourer, 1841-1912." *Irish Economic and Social History* 7 (1980): 66-92.

———. *Irish Emigration, 1801-1921*. Dublin: Dundalgan Press, 1984.

———. "Irish Emigration in the Later Nineteenth Century." *Irish Historical Studies* 22:86 (Sept. 1980): 126-43.

Harkness, D.A.E. "Irish Emigration." In *International Migrations*, vol. 2, edited by Walter F. Willcox and Imre Ferenczi, pp. 261-82. National Bureau for Economic Research. New York: Gordon and Breach, 1969.

Harris, Ruth-Ann. "Internal and External Migration as Alternatives: The Case of Pre-Famine Ireland." Boston, 1981. Mimeographed.

———. *The Search for Missing Friends: Irish Immigrant Advertisements Placed in the Boston "Pilot"*. Vol. I, *1831-1850*. Boston: New England Historical Genealogical Society, forthcoming.

Jackson, John Archer. *The Irish in Britain*. London: Routledge and Kegan Paul, 1963.

Jackson, Pauline. "Women in Nineteenth Century Irish Emigration." *International Migration Review* 18:4 (Winter 1984): 1004-20.

Lees, Lynn Hollen. *Exiles of Erin: Irish Migrants in Victorian London*. Ithaca, N.Y.: Cornell Univ. Press, 1979.

———. "Mid-Victorian Migration and the Irish Family Economy." *Victorian Studies* 20:1 (Autumn 1976): 25-43.

Lees, Lynn Hollen, and John Modell. "The Irish Countryman Urbanized: A Comparative Perspective on the Famine Migration." *Journal of Urban History* 3:4 (Aug. 1977): 391-408.

MacDonagh, Oliver. "Irish Emigration to the United States of America and the British Colonies During the Famine." In *The Great Famine: Studies in Irish History*, edited by Robert Dudley Edwards and T. Desmond Williams, pp. 317-88. New York: New York Univ. Press, 1957.

Mageean, Deirdre. "Nineteenth Century Irish Emigration: A Case Study Using Passenger Lists." In *The Irish in America: Emigration, Assimilation and Impact*, edited by P.J. Drudy, pp. 39-62. Irish Studies, no. 4. New York: Cambridge Univ. Press, 1985.

———. "Pre and Post Famine Migrant Families: Patterns and Change." Nashville, Tenn. 1981. Mimeographed.

Miller, Kerby A. *Emigrants and Exiles: Ireland and the Irish Exodus to North America*. New York: Oxford Univ. Press, 1985.

O'Grada, Cormac. "Seasonal Migration and Post-Famine Adjustment in the West of Ireland." *Studia Hibernica* 13 (1973): 48-76.

Oldham, C.H. "The Incidence of Emigration on Town and Country Life in Ireland." *Journal of the Statistical and Social Inquiry Society of Ireland* (pt. 94) 13 (Nov. 1913–June 1914): 207-18.

Schrier, Arnold. *Ireland and the American Emigration, 1850-1900*. New York: Russell and Russell, 1970.

Society

Akenson, Donald H. *The Irish Education Experiment: The National System of Education in the Nineteenth Century*. London: Routledge and Kegan Paul, 1970.

———. "National Education and the Realities of Irish Life, 1831-1900." *Eire-Ireland* 4:4 (Winter 1969): 42-51.

Arensberg, Conrad M., and Solon T. Kimball. *Family and Community in Ireland*. 2d ed. Cambridge: Harvard Univ. Press, 1968.

Bales, Robert F. "Attitudes toward Drinking in the Irish Culture." In *Society, Culture, and Drinking Patterns*, edited by David J. Pittman and Charles B. Snyder, pp. 157-87. New York: Wiley, 1962.

Boyle, John W. "A Marginal Figure: The Irish Rural Laborer." In *Irish Peasants: Violence and Political Protest, 1780-1914*, edited by Samuel Clark and James S. Donnelly, Jr., pp. 331-38. Madison: Univ. of Wisconsin Press, 1984.

Brody, Hugh. *Inishkillane: Change and Decline in the West of Ireland*. New York: Schocken Books, 1974.

Connell, K.H. *Irish Peasant Society: Four Historical Essays*. Oxford: Clarendon Press, 1968.

Connolly, Sean J. *Priests and People in Pre-Famine Ireland, 1780-1845*. Dublin: Gill and Macmillan, 1982.

Conway, Thomas G. "Women's Work in Ireland." *Eire-Ireland* 7:1 (1972): 10-27.

Corish, Patrick J. *The Irish Catholic Experience: A Historical Survey*. Dublin: Gill and Macmillan, 1982.

Council for the Status of Women (Ireland). *Irish Women Speak Out—A Plan of Action*. Dublin: Co-Op Books, 1981.

Crawford, E. Margaret. "Indian Meal and Pellagra in Nineteenth Century Ireland." In *Irish Population, Economy, and Society: Essays in Honour of the Late K.H. Connell*, edited by J.M. Goldstrom and L.A. Clarkson, pp. 112-33. New York: Oxford Univ. Press, 1981.

Cullen, L.M. *Life in Ireland*. New York: Putnam, 1968.

———. *Six Generations: Life and Work in Ireland from 1790*. Cork: Mercier, 1970.

Curtis, Lewis Perry, Jr. *Anglo-Saxons and Celts: A Study in Anti-Irish Prejudice in Victorian England*. Studies in British History and Culture, vol. 2. Bridgeport, Conn.: Conference on British Studies at the University of Bridgeport, 1968.

Daly, Mary E. "Women, Work and Trade Unionism." In *Women in Irish Society: The Historical Dimension,* edited by Margaret MacCurtain and Donncha O'Corrain, pp. 71-81. Westport, Conn.: Greenwood Press, 1979.

Evans, Estyn. "Peasant Beliefs in Nineteenth Century Ireland." In *Views of the Irish Peasantry, 1800-1916,* edited by Daniel J. Casey and Robert E. Rhodes, pp. 37-56. Hamden, Conn.: Archon Books, 1977.

Finegan, John. *The Story of Monto: An Account of Dublin's Notorious Red Light District.* Cork: Mercier Mini-Books, 1978.

Fortner, Robert S. "The Culture of Hope and the Culture of Despair: The Print Media and Nineteenth Century Irish Emigration." *Eire-Ireland* 13:3 (Fall 1978): 32-48.

Gilley, Sheridan. "English Attitudes toward the Irish, 1780-1900." In *Immigrants and Minorities in British Society,* edited by Colin Holmes, pp. 81-110. London: Allen and Unwin, 1978.

Goldschmidt, Walter, and Evalyn J. Kunkel. "The Structure of the Peasant Family." *American Anthropologist* 73:5 (Oct. 1971): 1058-76.

Goldstrom, J.M. *The Social Content of Education, 1808-1870: A Study of the Working-Class School Reader in England and Ireland.* Shannon: Irish Univ. Press, 1972.

Hannan, Damian. *Displacement and Development: Class, Kinship and Social Change in Irish Rural Communities.* Dublin, 1979.

Hannan, Damian, and L. Katsiaouni. *Traditional Families: From Culturally Prescribed to Negotiated Roles in Irish Farm Families.* Dublin, 1977.

Hogan, F. Edmund, S.J. *The Irish People: Their Height, Form, and Strength.* Dublin: M.H. Gill and Son, 1899.

Humphreys, Alexander J. *New Dubliners: Urbanization and the Irish Family.* London: Routledge and Kegan Paul, 1966.

Larkin, Emmet. "The Devotional Revolution in Ireland, 1850-1875." *American Historical Review* 77:3 (June 1972): 625-52.

——. *James Larkin: Irish Labour Leader, 1876-1947.* Cambridge: MIT Press, 1965.

——. *The Roman Catholic Church and the Creation of the Modern Irish State, 1878-1886.* Philadelphia: American Philosophical Society, 1975.

Lee, Joseph J. "Women and the Church Since the Famine." In *Women in Irish Society: The Historical Dimension,* edited by Margaret Mac-Curtain and Donncha O'Corrain, pp. 37-45. Westport, Conn.: Greenwood Press, 1979.

Lucy, Sean, ed. *Love Poems of the Irish.* Cork: Mercier Press, 1967.

MacCurtain, Margaret, and Donncha O'Corrain, eds. *Women in Irish*

Society: The Historical Dimension. Westport, Conn.: Greenwood Press, 1979.

———. "Women, the Vote and Revolution." In *Women in Irish Society: The Historical Dimension,* edited by Margaret MacCurtain and Donncha O'Corrain, pp. 46-57. Westport, Conn.: Greenwood Press, 1979.

MacLochlainn, Alf. "Gael and Peasant—A Case of Mistaken Identity?" In *Views of the Irish Peasantry, 1800-1916,* edited by Daniel J. Casey and Robert E. Rhodes, pp. 17-36. Hamden, Conn.: Archon Books, 1977.

Messenger, John C. *Inis Beag: Isle of Ireland.* New York: Holt, Rinehart and Winston, 1969.

———. "Sex and Repression in an Irish Folk Community." In *Human Sexual Behavior: Variations in the Ethnographic Spectrum,* edited by Donald S. Marshall and Robert C. Suggs, pp. 3-37. New York: Basic Books, 1971.

———. "Types and Causes of Disputes in an Irish Community." *Eire-Ireland* 3:111 (Fall 1968): 27-37.

Michaelson, Evalyn Jacobson, and Walter Goldschmidt. "Female Roles and Male Dominance among Peasants." *Southwestern Journal of Anthropology* 27:4 (Winter 1971): 330-52.

O'Brien, Joseph V. *'Dear, Dirty Dublin': A City in Distress, 1899-1916.* Berkeley: Univ. of California Press, 1982.

O'Danachair, Caoimhin. "The Dress of the Irish." *Eire-Ireland* 2:3 (Autumn 1967): 5-11.

O'Neill, Timothy. *Life and Tradition in Rural Ireland.* London: J.M. Dent and Sons, 1977.

O'Tuathaigh, Gearoid. "The Role of Women in Ireland under the New English Order." In *Women in Irish Society: The Historical Dimension,* edited by Margaret MacCurtain and Donncha O'Corrain, pp. 26-36. Westport, Conn.: Greenwood Press, 1979.

Waters, Martin J. "Peasants and Emigrants: Considerations of the Gaelic League as a Social Movement." In *Views of the Irish Peasantry, 1800-1916,* edited by Daniel J. Casey and Robert E. Rhodes, pp. 160-77. Hamden, Conn.: Archon Books, 1977.

Immigrant Women

Baum, Charlotte, Paula Hyman, and Sonya Michel. *The Jewish Woman in America.* New York: Dial, 1976.

Baxandall, Rosalyn, Linda Gordon, and Susan Reverby, eds. *America's Working Women.* New York: Random House, 1976.

Branca, Patricia, and Peter N. Stearns. *Modernization of Women in the Nineteenth Century*. St. Louis, Mo.: Forum Press, 1973.

Carpenter, Niles. *Immigrants and Their Children*. Census Monograph 7, 1927. New York: Arno, 1969.

Diner, Hasia. *Erin's Daughters in America: Irish Immigrant Women in the Nineteenth Century*. Baltimore: Johns Hopkins Univ. Press, 1983.

———. "Immigrant Women, Voluntary Associations, and the Process of Adaptation to Urban America." Cambridge, Mass. Mimeographed.

Donelin, Mary C. "American Irish Women 'Firsts.' " *American Irish Historical Society Journal* 24 (1925): 215-21.

Dublin, Thomas. *Women at Work: The Transformation of Work and Community in Lowell, Massachusetts, 1826-1860*. New York: Columbia Univ. Press, 1979.

Feldstein, Stanley, and Lawrence Costello, eds. *The Ordeal of Assimilation: A Documentary History of the White Working Class*. Garden City, N.Y.: Anchor, 1974.

Fink, Gary W. *Biographical Dictionary of American Labor*. Westport, Conn.: Greenwood Press, 1984.

Glanz, Rudolf. *The Jewish Woman in America: Two Female Immigrant Generations, 1820-1929*. Vol. 1, *The Eastern European Jewish Woman*. KTAV Publishing House and the National Council of Jewish Women, 1976.

———. *The Jewish Woman in America: Two Immigrant Female Generations, 1820-1929*. Vol. 2, *The German Jewish Woman*. KTAV Publishing House and the National Council of Jewish Women, 1976.

Greenwald, Maurine Weiner. *Women, War, and Work: The Impact of World War I on Women Workers in the United States*. Westport, Conn.: Greenwood Press, 1979.

Handlin, Oscar. *The Uprooted: The Epic Story of the Great Migrations That Made the American People*. New York: Grosset and Dunlap, 1951.

Hutchinson, Edward P. *Immigrants and Their Children, 1850-1950*. Social Science Research Council, U.S. Department of Commerce, Bureau of the Census. New York: Wiley, 1956.

Katzman, David M. *Seven Days a Week: Women and Domestic Service in Industrializing America*. New York: Oxford Univ. Press, 1978.

Kenneally, James J. *Women and American Trade Unions*. St. Albans, Vt.: Eden Press Women's Publications, 1978.

Kessner, Thomas. *The Golden Door: Italian and Jewish Immigrant Mobility in New York City, 1880-1915*. New York: Oxford Univ. Press, 1977.

Krause, Corinne Azen. "Urbanization without Breakdown: Italian, Jewish, and Slavic Immigrant Women in Pittsburgh, 1900-1945." *Journal of Urban History* 4:3 (May 1978): 291-306.

Kraut, Alan M. *The Huddled Masses: The Immigrant in American Society, 1880-1921.* Arlington Heights, Ill.: Harlan Davidson, 1982.

Ljungmark, Lars. *Swedish Exodus.* Translated by Kermit B. Westerberg. Carbondale: Southern Illinois Univ. Press, 1979.

Nelli, Humbert S. "Ethnic Group Assimilation: The Italian Experience." In *Cities in American History,* edited by Kenneth T. Jackson and Stanley K. Schultz, pp. 199-215. New York: Knopf, 1972.

O'Dea, John. *History of the Ancient Order of Hibernians and Ladies' Auxiliary.* Philadelphia: National Board of the A.O.H., 1923.

O'Grady, John. *Catholic Charities in the United States: History and Problems.* Washington, D.C.: National Conference of Catholic Charities, 1930; New York: Arno Press, 1971.

Rischen, Moses. *The Promised City: New York's Jews, 1870-1914.* New York: Harper Torchbooks, 1962.

Salmon, Lucy Maynard. *Domestic Service.* New York: Macmillan, 1897.

Scarpaci, Jean, ed. "Immigrant Women in the City—Introduction." *Journal of Urban History* 4:3 (May 1978): 251-53.

Scott, Joan, and Louise Tilly. "Women's Work and the Family in Nineteenth Century Europe." *Comparative Studies in Society and History* 17:1 (Jan. 1975): 36-64.

Seller, Maxine. "Beyond the Stereotype: A New Look at the Immigrant Woman, 1880-1924." *Journal of Ethnic Studies* 3:1 (Spring 1975): 59-70.

———. "The Education of the Immigrant Woman: 1900 to 1935." *Journal of Urban History* (May 1978): 307-30.

Shorter, Edward. "Female Emancipation, Birth Control and Fertility in European History." *American Historical Review* 78:3 (June 1973): 605-40.

Steinberg, Stephen. *The Ethnic Myth: Race, Ethnicity, and Class in America.* New York: Atheneum, 1981.

Streib, Gordon F. "Old Age in Ireland: Demographic and Sociological Aspects." *Gerontologist* 8:4 (Winter 1968): 227-35.

Sullerot, Evelyne. *Women, Society and Change.* Translated by Margaret Scotford Archer. New York: McGraw-Hill, 1971.

Tilly, Louise A., and Joan W. Scott. *Women, Work, and the Family.* New York: Holt, Rinehart and Winston, 1978.

Tilly, Louise A., Joan W. Scott, and Miriam Cohen. "Women's Work and European Fertility Patterns." *Journal of Interdisciplinary History* 6:3 (Winter 1976): 447-76.

Vecoli, Rudolph J. " 'Contadini' in Chicago: A Critique of *The Uprooted.*" *Journal of American History* 51:3 (Dec. 1964): 404-17.

Weatherford, Doris. *Foreign and Female: Immigrant Women in America, 1840-1930.* New York: Schocken Books, 1986.

Yans-McLaughlin, Virginia. *Family and Community: Italian Immigrants in Buffalo, 1880-1930.* Ithaca, N.Y.: Cornell Univ. Press, 1977.

———. "A Flexible Tradition: South Italian Immigrants Confront a New York Experience." *Journal of Social History* 7:4 (Summer 1974): 429-45.

———. "Patterns of Work and Family Organization: Buffalo's Italians." *Journal of Interdisciplinary History* 2:2 (Autumn 1971): 299-314.

Index

agricultural laborers: as percentage of the population, 11, 15, 36, 52; impact of population change on, 23, 58; impact of land reform on, 60; women as, 61-62, 64

Ancient Order of Hibernians, 85-87

Arensberg, Conrad, 6

Barry, Leonora, 84

Belfast, 18, 21, 66; women's employment opportunities in, 62; mortality rates in, 66. *See also* urbanization

British government: impact on Irish economy, 11, 14; awareness of Irish poverty, 18; impact on Irish education, 39. *See also* land reform; national schools

cash economy, 14, 21, 33, 71; and credit and bank deposits, 21, 59-60; women's earnings in, 30-31, 62-63; and incomes, 44, 59, 61. *See also* economy

church (Catholic), 27, 28, 85; and Catholic population, 29; attendance, 29, 36-37; as agency of social control, 29, 36; attitude toward women, 36; in the US, 87; women's financial contribution to, 87; as center of women's social life, 88. *See also* nuns

communication: emigrant letters, 5, 42; penny post, 41; periodicals, 41-42

cultural values: about marriage, 42, 73-74; and material aspirations, 42, 73-74; after emigration, 85-86, 89. *See also* popular culture

Diner, Hasia, 6

domestic industry, 18, 31, 44; demise of, 31, 34, 62

domestic service, 28, 63-64; women's attitudes toward, 37, 67-69, 74, 78, 82-84, 94; working conditions in, 63, 78-79, 94; in foreign cities, 67-68, 78, 83, 94

Donovan, Mary Ann. *See* Nolan, Mary Ann Donovan

dowries, 33-34

Dublin, 21; women's employment opportunities in, 62-65; mortality rates in, 65-66; overcrowding in, 66. *See also* urbanization